F

Heaven

What Golf Can Teach Us About Our Catholic Faith and the Sacraments

By
R. J. Gilson

Fairway to Heaven
What Golf Can Teach Us About Our Catholic Faith
and the Sacraments

Copyright© 2025 by R.J. Gilson

ISBN: 979-8-218-74408-3

Published by
Richard Gilson
Jonestown, PA

Cover Design: www.emilysworldofdesign.com

Dedication

The book is lovingly, graciously, and sincerely dedicated to:

My wife Carolyn and our awesome 43 years and counting. Our life together has been blessed in countless ways, from our chance meeting on a softball field in Carlisle, PA to our nine grandchildren.

Our four children, Tarah, Stephanie, Joseph and Matthew. All are now grown up and have embarked on journeys of their own.

Our nine grandchildren. They are all still so young, but we can see a bright future for each of them.

Talia, the first grandchild, already possesses every tool to be whatever she puts her mind to. Dominic has smarts and determination; he's a thinker. Anthony has learned from his siblings and can be the best of both. Jackson is as smart as he is fast. I'm known as *GPG* because he said Grandpa G so fast, that is how it sounded. Reagan— my little sweet pea—is our social butterfly; she loves everyone. Kennedy has that "Strausie" look and the personality to match. Grant is way too young, but he is such a chill baby; still not sure I've ever heard him cry. Whitney is still our Baby Whitney, but she is cute as a button and very smart. Charlie is only a few months old and is the first of his generation to continue the family name.

Last but not least, there are three very special ladies. Barbara, Kay, and Vickie. These women formed a foundational bridge that spanned my working career. Without them, I have no career.

Sadly, my brother-in-law Steve passed away during the writing of this book. Steve was my first proofreader, he inspired the title, was my biggest supporter, and provided enormous amounts of encouragement for this project.

If I were to die tomorrow, what could I possibly complain about?

Table of Contents

Introduction

An athletic endeavor is a wonderful thing. Virtually all sports, organized or not, do wonders for the body and soul. Beyond the obvious: physical fitness, fellowship, teamwork, goal setting, sports help us stretch our capacities for strength and endurance, planning and execution, working as a team or even as individuals. Much of what we do when we participate in sports, such as learning the technical aspects, training, playing, and even handling the results of the competition—winning and losing—is indeed transferable to our daily lives, both physical and spiritual. Sports have an ultimate goal: Kick the ball into the net, score more runs or points than your opponent, and get the ball into the hole. Life has a goal too: Get to Heaven.

My Journey, My Story

I love reading or hearing about conversion stories. They are often sensational, like Scott Hahn's compelling story in his book, *Rome Sweet Home.* I particularly like to read about the various saints and their stories. Francis of Assisi, Augustine, and Mother Teresa come to mind. My story, not so much. My story is more slog than a splash, but here it is....

I am a cradle Catholic, the sixth of ten children, and a foster brother; spellbinding stuff, right? The foundation for my faith was solid. My parents were active and engaged Catholics. Mom bore the brunt of child-rearing, the day-to-day household activity, while Dad was working. She did tend to spoil us. We all felt like we were her favorite. To this day, and we are all in our 60's and 70's now, we'll banter about; each of us providing some proof of being the favorite son or daughter. Up until now, no one has provided indisputable proof of "favorite" status. I usually stay quiet during these debates because I knew early on, it was I who was the true favorite.

Parenting was a solid partnership for Mom and Dad, but when we strayed from the good path, and discipline was warranted, Mom tried very hard, but it usually resulted in more laughter than crying. She usually deferred the serious issues to Dad. My father was a true disciplinarian, and he was very good at it. To hear the words, "Just wait until your father gets home," would strike fear into the hearts of all of us.

My father couldn't have done much more for our parish. He was a member of The Holy Name Society, and St. Vincent de Paul. He ushered at Mass, counted the collection, and attended most every committee meeting. As a meat cutter at the local grocery store, he often provided catering for most dinner/dance events and even directed traffic in the parking lot.

The church parking lot was where I learned to drive. Dad would load up the back of our station wagon with old wooden parking barricades (glorified sawhorses) and it was my job to steer straight ahead and step on the brake every ten or twenty yards so he could take a barricade off and place it strategically on the blacktop. Later, we used an old 1949 GMC pickup truck, and I was able to learn to drive a stick shift—three on the tree—all before I was 12 years old. Great memories.

We were brought up in the Church the right way. Most of my siblings were schooled at the parish school through eighth grade. The oldest two boys and three oldest sisters attended Catholic high schools. Tuition became too cumbersome for the rest of us, so we transferred to the public high schools. We received the Sacraments in an orderly manner, including Baptism, Reconciliation (also called Confession), Eucharist, and Confirmation. I became an altar boy in fourth grade, back in the day when you had to learn Latin to be eligible to serve. I failed my first tryout, but once I passed the test, I was off and running. I would often hang around the church on

Sundays just to get the opportunity to serve at Mass if another altar boy didn't show up. It was not uncommon for me to serve at several Masses on any given Sunday.

During my high school years from 1967-1971, a new Christian evangelical movement was becoming prevalent. This movement was generally described as groups of born-again Christians, or less respectfully, "Jesus Freaks." The unofficial image of this movement was the wild rainbow-colored wig worn by a sports fan holding up a "John 3:16" sign. Arguably, this campaign firmly established John 3:16: *For God so loved the world, that he gave his only begotten Son, that whosoever believeth in him should not perish, but have everlasting life,* as the most popular, or at the very least, the most well-known verse in the Bible.

It was a strange time for Catholics in my age group. It was a very intense period. These "Jesus Freaks" would be in your face and sometimes very aggressive in their approach to evangelization. I would often find myself sharing a table with some high school friends, typically involving me and three former Catholics. This is where I first remembered being an Apologetic (defender of the faith). Even the word "apologetics," wasn't frequently used, at least not in my world. Our table conversations generally revolved around the things that Catholics did or "believed," but my friends disagreed with—man made rules, crazy rituals, etc. As I think back and reminisce about these conversations, a quote from Venerable Archbishop Fulton Sheen seemed to sum up the sentiment nicely.

"There are not one hundred people in the United States who hate the Catholic Church, but there are millions who hate what they wrongly perceive the Catholic Church to be."[1]

I wasn't an expert on Catholicism by any stretch, so my defense of the Church was limited and mostly ineffectual. As time passed, this movement settled down a bit, and the tone of their message

---

[1] FultonSheen.com

became less aggressive; I remember two distinct takeaways from these table discussions. First, even though I may not have known the answer to many of their questions, I knew my parents would not lie to me about what Catholics believe. And second, I was determined to learn all that I could about the Catholic Church.

My journey to learn more about my Catholic faith started very slowly at first. I began by reading pamphlets and a few short books on the subject, but spiritually, my high school and college years were mostly filled with idleness. I went to Mass nearly every Sunday—my faith foundation was solid enough for me to maintain obedience to the Third Commandment—but these years were spent mostly trying to graduate college and find my career. I was "checking boxes," as they say.

During the early years of our marriage, I credit my wife, Carolyn, for keeping me on the rails spiritually. It would have been easy for me to rationalize my way out of going to Mass. After all, I worked hard and traveled often, and Saturday evenings were a time to relax or perhaps do some late-night socializing. Sleeping in on Sundays would've been a great way to enjoy some downtime and get ready for the rushed work-a-day grind that was just a few hours away. Carolyn's gentle nudges were just enough to keep my fragile little salvation wagon on the trail.

I thank God for her gentle nudges. Even though I may have been "checking the boxes," I was serious about "keeping holy the Sabbath."[2] It is His Commandment, and not a suggestion. What little our God asks of us but to commit an hour a week (at the very minimum) to formally come and give thanks to Him and to receive Him, Body, Blood, Soul, and Divinity, in the Eucharist. What a special gift!

We followed our parents' example and committed to sending our children to Catholic schools. As they got old enough to participate

---

[2] Deut 5:12. Holy Bible. The Great Adventure Bible, Revised Standard Version, Second Catholic Edition.

in travel soccer and other sports, we made sure we always attended Sunday Mass, even if we were out of town for tournaments. This, too, created many great memories—attending new and different churches, family breakfasts in out-of-town diners, and way too many fleabag motels (literally fleas, bedbugs, we saw it all).

That First Bible Study

Fast forward to 2005. I joined a parish Bible study, "From Genesis to Jesus," and my faith journey was kicked up a notch. It was like the old car battery was put on a charger. What followed this Bible study was a slow, steady stream of faith enrichment. I joined the Knights of Columbus. I read a book, bought a book, bought another book, went back to confession (after nearly 30 years of absence), attended a silent retreat, joined the pastoral council, joined the Cursillo movement, became an Extraordinary Minister of Holy Communion (EMHC), joined more parish activities, and conducted Bible studies. The journey, one hundred percent inspired by the Holy Spirit, continues today. May the Lord be praised!

This journey has produced much fruit. It wouldn't be inaccurate to describe my faith journey as an old gas range with a pilot light lit but only flickering until that first Bible study. That's when *Someone* turns on a burner, then another burner, then another. Much of my formation in the past twenty years has actually been a refresher course in what I had been taught as a youth, but never quite took "root." I experienced many "aha" moments along the way. This book includes many such moments. Moments that involved the similarities of sports and spiritual life, particularly the game of golf.

One such moment came as I was concluding an adult Bible study on the Sacraments. As I was preparing for the final session, a review of all seven Sacraments, the similarities between the sacraments and the game of golf hit me like a ton of bricks. The similarities were staggering. In my view, all sports contribute to our well-being, but for my money, no sport mirrors the aspects of our journey toward salvation more than the game of golf.

5

Growing up with Catholic teaching, almost as often as you hear the word catholic, you also hear its meaning: that the word catholic means universal. Universal in the sense that it is affecting or done by all people. So, proclaiming that golf is a little "c" catholic is not a hugely profound statement. After all, golf is a worldwide sport open to all who wish to participate; golf literally welcomes all people. But to proclaim that the game of golf is big "C" Catholic, now that is a truly bold proclamation. In these pages, I will make the case that golf is Catholicism at its core, and the Seven Sacraments are thoroughly imbedded into every aspect of the game, from tee to green. We'll dissect this beautiful and very challenging game and uncover the hidden gems—the Sacraments—that not only prepare us to live our lives more joyfully but help us to cooperate in God's grace more fully.

Author's Disclaimer:

Any comparison with aspects of the game of golf to official Church teaching is not intended to equate these aspects to official Church teaching. These comparisons are mostly tongue-in-cheek, and are intended to draw some parallels with Church teaching, especially with respect to the Sacraments.

ONE
The Garden Of Eden

(The Sacraments)

"In the beginning, God created the heavens and the earth."[3] God didn't stop there. "And God said, 'Let the earth put forth vegetation, plants yielding seed, and fruit trees bearing fruit in which is their seed, each according to its kind, upon the earth.' *And it was so*…And God saw that it was good."[4] ***The first golf course.***

A couple of days later, as the story continues, God created man. Not an insignificant event. God gave the man, later to be known as Adam, a job. "The LORD God took the man and put him in the garden of Eden to till it and keep it."[5] Adam was essentially "hired" to maintain the Garden and keep its pristine condition. ***The first golf course superintendent.***

Adam was not only the first superintendent but also the physical and spiritual leader of his new family. In scripture, he was frequently represented "in the tradition of rabbinic interpretation as a priest."[6] A priest is predominantly a teacher and servant, ***the first golf professional.***

"And the LORD God commanded the man, saying, 'you may freely eat of every tree in the garden; but of the tree of the knowledge of good and evil you shall not eat.'"[7] ***The first Rules of Golf.***

When we experience a golf course, particularly the pristine, well-manicured masterpieces like Augusta National, the

---

[3] Gn 1:1. Holy Bible. The Great Adventure Bible, Revised Standard Version, Second Catholic Edition.

[4] Gn 1:11-13.

[5] Gn 2:15.

[6] Bishop Robert Barron, *This is My Body; A Call to Eucharistic Revival, (Word on Fire, 2023)*.

[7] Gn 2:16-17.

comparisons to God's Garden of Eden are undeniable. The air is fresh and clean. There is usually a myriad of wildlife, trees, lakes, ponds, and creeks, not to mention beautiful, lush green grass. The Rules of Golf dictate that we "keep it" that way. The signs in and around the course are abundantly clear: replace divots, cart path only, rake the sand traps, and repair pitch marks. Additionally, the Rules direct us to even protect our fellow "stewards" by yelling "FORE" after a wayward shot dangerously heads toward them.

"Then the LORD God said, 'It is not good that a man should be alone; I will make him a helper fit for him.'…she shall be called woman."[8] Adam and Eve thus became *the first two-some.*

Although the initial "helpers" mentioned in Scripture were "beasts of the field and every bird of the air"[9], it is not lost on those of us who golf, that your golf partner is an invaluable "help" as you proceed through your round. Your golf partner is often relied on to watch the flight of your ball, help determine the proper interpretation of the Rules, and, on perhaps way too many occasions, give advice. In my experience, my golf partners have been terrific examples of fellowship, encouragement, and good laughs.

Who is Your Adam and Eve?

Golf, as it imitates life, is primarily an individual sport, but it is not really meant to be played alone. Practically speaking, it is almost essential that someone else watches us swing and helps keep an eye on the ball, especially if your ball doesn't hit the fairway.

My first partners were the El Fados (sorry, Carolyn, you weren't the first). The El Fados have a long history, beginning with our high school football team. There is a large book waiting to be written about the El Fados, but for this book, it is sufficient to give you a brief bit of background and an introduction to the more notable characters involved in this large chapter of my life.

The origins of the El Fados began with Mr. Cagle, coach of the receivers. Coach Cagle named this group of receivers, The El Fados. It was his job to mold a group of misfit toys into a formidable team of pass receivers. The results on the practice field looked like coach Cagle was trying his best to herd a bunch of feral cats—or better yet

---

[8] Gn 2:18,23.
[9] Gn 2:19.

trying to nail Jello to a wall. There are too many caricatures of Coach Cagle to mention, but to be completely fair to him, he did try very hard. If you've ever seen the television series, *Monk*, Coach Cagle would have nailed the role of Lieutenant Disher. Cagle did have, within this collection of extremely ADHD-afflicted misfits, a group of highly skilled, sure-handed, very fast, and very talented pass catchers. One of them actually went on to play at BYU and still holds NCAA pass-receiving records.

The de facto leader of this group of misfits was unquestionably David. David's leadership can best be described as "leading from the rear." His talent was taking innocent, unassuming, normal people, like me and Dennis, and coercing us to do inane things, such as fall down ornate staircases in fancy hotels, climb very tall electrical towers at pre-dawn hours, or ascend the letters of "Ghirardelli" in San Francisco to remove a kite stuck on the "G". He actually convinced his sister Ellen to do that. Always harmless, if you discount the danger involved, which we almost always did, but always borderline insanity. Adult beverages may have been involved, but that was never proven. David's skill was vanishing into the background as things tended to go horribly wrong. Ken and Kirk were also part of the original El Fados and together, the five of us have survived and persevered in our brotherhood. Ken and Kirk are arguably the sanest of the bunch, but we can debate about that later.

So, while the exploits of the El Fados will largely go unmentioned here, David, Dennis, Ken, and I played a bit of golf early in my senior year of high school. During one of my very first rounds of golf, I got my first birdie, on the eighth hole at Sunken Gardens in Santa Clara, CA. It was not the conventional one-putt birdie, in fact, it wasn't a birdie at all. I hit my tee shot on the par 3 and the ball landed on a big black crow standing next to the green. Sadly, the crow didn't survive, but my story did. This might end up being a metaphor for my entire golf career.

Not all of my golf partners have been, shall we say, as eccentric as the El Fados. My most favored partner is Carolyn, of course. She can be a bit of an enigma at times, but it is thoroughly enjoyable to golf with her and we have lots of fun. We golf with some dear friends, Craig and Cindy. Craig and I need to bring "Quiet Please" signs next time we play with the ladies. The girls talk constantly from tee to green, but it is always a hoot playing with them.

In recent years, I've been especially grateful to play with Greg, a great friend from church. He is thoroughly enjoyable and fun to play with. We tend to solve all of our problems during the round. From grandkids to church events, everything is better by the time we reach the 18th green; if not, we continue our problem-solving at the 19th hole. Greg is the one partner who keeps my impatience in check. He has such an even temper when he plays, and sometimes it rubs off on me. It is such a blessing and joy to play the game the way he does. I need to do what he does, every round.

It is a total pleasure to be able to golf with family. Our two boys and one of our daughters have taken up the game, too. Matthew is by far the gold standard in golfing skills, Joseph has the skill but just needs more time on the course, and Tarah is just beginning but hits it a ton "for a girl." Our other daughter, Stephanie, and daughter-in-law, Savanna, do not play. They are both blessed with athletic abilities, but we can't entice them enough to give it a go. Steph actually tried once with her siblings, but she woke up the next day with a sore back, so she's probably done. The two sons-in-law, Chris and Mike, also play, and they both hit the ball a mile off the tee.

My brothers get into the act as well. Years ago, when all of my brothers played, we would make sure to put a round of golf on the agenda whenever we all got together. Little brothers Berk and Robbie are the best of the bunch, although Robbie is still head and shoulders above the rest of us. Even now, Berk, who lives near Nashville, Matthew, Carolyn, and I will meet halfway, about five hours for each of us, to play a round, then return home, sometimes the same day.

So, even though we are ultimately judged individually, life in the Garden and life on the golf course is so much more fulfilling, rewarding, and pleasurable when shared with one another.

The Sacraments in Golf

Before we immerse ourselves further, it is time to introduce the Sacraments as described by the Catechism of the Catholic Church:

"Christ instituted the sacraments of the new law. There are seven: Baptism, Confirmation, the Eucharist, Penance, the Anointing of the Sick, Holy Orders, and Matrimony. The seven sacraments touch all the stages and all the important moments of

Christian life: they give birth and increase, healing and mission to the Christian's life of faith. There is thus a certain resemblance between the stages of natural life and the stages of the spiritual life."[10]

Baptism 'is birth into the new life of Christ."[11] Confirmation strengthens and "perfects Baptismal grace."[12] The Eucharist "nourished us with Christ's Body and Blood."[13] Penance forgives our sins and reconciles us to God.[14] The Anointing of the Sick, among other graces, is "the preparation for passing over to eternal life."[15] "Holy Orders and Matrimony are directed toward the salvation of others."[16]

All sacraments, to be valid, must include three elements specific to each particular sacrament: Formula, Matter, and Intention. The Form is generally the prayers of the ordinary ministers, the Matter is a tangible thing or action, and the Intention, the will to do what the Church does in each sacrament, is required by the ministers of the sacrament as well as those that the sacrament is being conferred upon.

The game of golf also mirrors many of the same stages of natural life, does it not? Starting as a youth, we'll naturally begin with a junior set of clubs. The tee box is moved up for juniors. As we get older and more skilled, we grow into a regular set of clubs and tee off from the regular tees, whites or blues generally. As we get older and become seniors, we'll use the gold tee box.

As you dive deeper into this book, you'll see how golf is closely related to the sacraments. For example, starting with the sacraments of initiation, Baptism, Confirmation, and the Eucharist, we'll join the club, grow in wisdom, and be nourished at every turn. In the sacraments of healing, Reconciliation and Anointing of the Sick, we'll receive forgiveness for our bad shots. The sacraments of service, Holy Orders and Matrimony, will help us appreciate

---

[10] CCC ¶ 1210.
[11] CCC ¶ 1277.
[12] CCC ¶ 1316.
[13] CCC ¶ 1316.
[14] CCC ¶ 1422 (paraphrased).
[15] CCC ¶ 1532.
[16] CCC ¶ 1534.

lifelong partnerships and fellowship.

So the table is set, as they say. The "Garden" is ready. Good and fertile soil, lush green grass, abundant trees, and other foliage, rules to help us maintain the garden, a teacher to help us succeed and attain our "goal," friends and family to assist along the way. The next steps for us include our promise and commitment to work toward the goal, get the ball into the hole, or better yet, get your soul into Heaven!

TWO
Welcome to the Club

(Baptism)

For some very exclusive private golf clubs, membership and entrance into the club is sometimes a matter of birthright. You don't really need any special skills to be granted membership. The same is true for non-exclusive public courses, no special skills are needed. Granted, you'll need some amount of cash to play golf, a rather large sum of cash to play at private clubs, but cash requirements aside, a person can reasonably argue that it is by the grace of God (sometimes grace can take the form of sponsorship by others) that you can walk up to the first tee and "BE" a golfer. One can also reasonably argue that to be considered as a member of the golfing community only requires the intention to be a golfer. So, you don't need to be a good golfer, you don't even need to be a golfer, but to gain access to the course, you need to be a member of the club.

In many respects, the Sacrament of Baptism can be described as the process of becoming a member of the club—the Christian Club. Just as a golf club membership is necessary to gain access to the golf course, and thereby achieving the main goal of getting the ball into the hole at the end of the process, the Church maintains that to achieve our main goal of getting to Heaven (Salvation), "Baptism is necessary for salvation for those to whom the Gospel has been proclaimed and who have had the possibility of asking for this sacrament." The Lord himself, "affirms that Baptism is necessary for salvation."[17] "Jesus answered, 'Truly, truly, I say to you unless one is born of water and the Spirit, he cannot enter the kingdom of

---

[17] CCC ¶1257.

God'"[18]

"Baptism is the basis of the whole Christian life, the gateway to life in the Spirit, and the door which gives access to the other Sacraments."[19] Baptism is not repeated. It is essentially a lifetime membership in the club. It "is God's most beautiful and magnificent gift…It is called a *gift* because it is conferred on those who bring nothing of their own."[20]

So, knowing the ultimate objective in the game of golf is to get the golf ball into the hole, can we reasonably connect the golf ball to our eternal soul and the hole to Heaven? Of course, we can!

In Christian circles, there is a seemingly endless debate on salvation. How are we saved? Are we saved once or a thousand times? Do we earn our entrance into Heaven? Certainly, since the time of Jesus, both Christian and non-Christian alike, have asked the question: "Teacher, what must I do to have eternal life (salvation)?"[21] Perhaps a reason the question of salvation is the subject of endless debate is that even in Scripture, there are seemingly many answers to that question. What the Catholic Church says about the biblical plan for salvation can be summarized nicely by this post from *Catholic Answers*:

"The saving grace won by Jesus is offered as a free gift to us, accessible through repentance, faith, and baptism… Good works are required by God because he requires obedience to his commands, and promises to reward us with eternal life if we obey. But even our obedience is impossible without God's grace; even our good works are God's gift. This is the real biblical plan of salvation."[22]

So, the short answer, and the one most simply stated, is that we are saved by the Grace of God. But the point of this book isn't so much about having a debate about salvation as it is seeing the sacraments, as instituted by Jesus, displayed so vividly in this wonderful game of golf.

---

[18] Jn 3:5. The Holy Bible, Revised Standard Version, 2nd Edition. The Great Adventure Bible.

[19] CCC ¶1213.

[20] CCC ¶1216.

[21] Mt 19:16. The Holy Bible, Revised Standard Version, 2nd Edition. The Great Adventure Bible.

[22] Catholic Answers, *What Is the Catholic Understanding of the Biblical Plan of Salvation?*.

After His resurrection, Jesus gave the Apostles this Sacrament of Baptism, for the purpose of giving it to us: "Go therefore and make disciples of all nations, baptizing them in the name of the Father and of the Son and of the Holy Spirit, teaching them to observe all that I have commanded you."[23]

"Baptism seals the Christian with the indelible spiritual mark of his belonging to Christ. No sin can erase this mark."[24] Similarly, as we wear the merchandise of the golf club— hats, sweaters, bag tags—pay our dues and assessments, and socialize at gatherings— all the things that identify us as members of the club. Can we relate Baptism to "joining the club"? Hmmm, I'm thinking, Yes!

Promises, Commitments, and Responsibilities

When you join a golf club, you've also made a huge commitment, both in time and treasure. The larger and more prestigious the club, the larger the commitment. There are mandatory initiation fees, monthly minimums, food and drink requirements, etc. You are responsible for paying these fees for as long as you maintain the relationship with the club, but all of these commitments and responsibilities come with a promise as well. If you do all that is asked and you participate fully, your chances for success in the game of golf are very high.

Baptism also involves promises, commitments, and responsibilities. "Baptism is the sacrament of faith. But faith needs the community of believers... The faith required for Baptism is not a perfect and mature faith, but a beginning that is called to develop."[25] "For all the baptized, children or adults, faith must grow *after* Baptism."[26]

The community of believers in the golf world are the other members of the club. The members, including the golf professional, assist in your "growth" and progress as a golfer. In life and the Christian's faith journey, parents and godparents are vital components in this process of growing faith.

The Catechism does a wonderful job describing the free gift

---

[23] Mt 28:19-20.
[24] CCC ¶ 1272.
[25] CCC ¶ 1253.
[26] CCC ¶ 1254.

of grace inherent with the Christian "membership" process. "Baptism not only purifies from all sins, but also makes the neophyte 'a new creature,' an adopted son of God, who has become a 'partaker of the divine nature,' member of Christ and co-heir with him, and a temple of the Holy Spirit."[27] The Catechism declares this grace in ¶1266:

"The Most Holy Trinity gives the baptized sanctifying grace, the grace of justification:

- enabling them to believe in God, to hope in him, and to love him through the theological virtues;
- giving them the power to live and act under the prompting of the Holy Spirit through the gifts of the Holy Spirit;
- allowing them to grow in goodness through moral virtues.

Thus the whole organism of the Christian's supernatural life has its roots in Baptism."[28]

The golfing world can't match the Christian initiation, but on its own merits, we can see some relatable comparisons, not the least of which is a bond of unity between its members. "Baptism constitutes the foundation of communion among all Christians. Justified by faith in Baptism, they are incorporated into Christ; they therefore have a right to be called Christians, and with good reason are accepted as brothers by the children of the Catholic Church. Baptism therefore constitutes the sacramental bond of unity existing among all who through it are reborn."[29]

So, fulfilling our Baptismal promises has a two-fold meaning: As parents and godparents, we promised to raise the new child of God in the faith, through instruction, formation, and being good living examples of Christ, as does the club membership and others promise the support and guidance for the new members. The second meaning of the Baptismal promise is the promise of salvation, well, the salvation in the golf world is the promise of great scores and perhaps even a trophy or two.

---

[27] CCC ¶ 1265.
[28] CCC ¶ 1266.
[29] CCC ¶ 1271.

This is a first step in our required obedience to God and a step "necessary for salvation".[30] Congratulations!

---

[30] CCC ¶ 1257.

Did You Know?

"The ordinary ministers of Baptism are the bishop, and priest and, in the Latin Church, also the deacon."[31] But, did you know, "In case of necessity, anyone, even a non-baptized person, with the required intention, can baptize."[32] Remembering that all sacraments must have Form, Matter and Intent to be a valid sacrament, the Form for Baptism is, "(Name of the person to be baptized), I baptize you in the name of the Father, and of the Son, and of the Holy Spirit."[33] The Matter is the water, "that he pours on the candidates head,"[34] and, "the intention required is to will to do what the Church does when she baptizes."[35]

---

[31] CCC ¶ 1256.
[32] CCC ¶ 1256.
[33] CCC ¶ 1240.
[34] CCC ¶ 1284.
[35] CCC ¶ 1256.

THREE
The Pro Shop

(Holy Orders)

The next logical step for us new or "reborn" golfers is education—golf lessons, training, and fundamental formation. After we have joined the club, we could actually just wander out to the first tee and whack away, right? Well yes, but our probability of success would be slim to none. We need help. We need instruction, equipment, clothing—we need lots of help. Our first stop should be a visit to the pro shop. The pro shop is where you'll find the golf professional. The professional can provide proper lessons on how to actually play and enjoy the game. You'll learn proper grip, stance, and swing plane. You'll learn to hit irons and woods, how to use the putter, and how to chip. Part of your instruction will include the development of good practice habits, using the driving range to hit a bucket of balls, practice chipping and putting, stretching and fitness. You'll even learn proper golf etiquette. Golf lessons are invaluable to your growth as a golfer. The golf professional's service to others is directed toward the salvation of golfers: ultimately, getting the ball into the hole in the fewest possible strokes. Lessons can start at an early age or later in life. If you take up the game of golf as a youth, the lessons you receive will generally follow your physical growth and mental development. As you grow, the equipment you use and the strategies you'll learn will appropriately follow your physical development.

The Sacrament of Holy Orders (the priesthood) is "directed toward the salvation of others; if they contribute as well to personal salvation, it is through service to others that they do so."[36] Are the

---

[36] CCC ¶ 1534.

similarities between the golf professional and the clergy simply a coincidence? Hmmm, I think not.

The priesthood, consisting of the episcopate (bishops), presbyterate (priests), and diaconate (deacons), is all about service to others. These three degrees of priesthood provide for our formation and assist us throughout our journey toward salvation— getting the ball (our souls) into the hole (heaven).

Golf professionals have unique and specialized training. Where does the priesthood come from? Well, it goes way back. As mentioned before, Adam was frequently mentioned in the traditional interpretation of the priestly role. God spoke to the Israelites at Mount Sinai, saying, "And you shall be to me a kingdom of priests and a holy nation."[37] Isaiah adds, "You shall be called the priests of the Lord, men shall speak of you as the ministers of our God."[38] As the Catechism states, "But within the people of Israel, God chose one of the twelve tribes, that of Levi, and set it apart for liturgical service."[39]

The Catechism further explains, "Everything that the priesthood of the Old Covenant prefigured finds its fulfillment in Christ Jesus, the "one mediator between God and men." The Christian tradition considers Melchizedek, "priest of God Most High", a prefiguration of the (one) priesthood of Christ." [40]

So, going back to the very first human, we are all called to be priests (teachers). This priesthood is commonly referred to as a baptismal or common priesthood of the faithful, part of our baptismal promises, what we committed to at Baptism. In the case of infant baptism, our parents or guardians made this commitment for us. The common priesthood "participate with the ministerial priesthood (bishops, priests, deacons), each in its own proper way, in the one priesthood of Christ. While being ordered one to another, they differ essentially. In what sense? While the common priesthood of the faithful is exercised by the unfolding of baptismal grace, a life of faith, hope, and charity, a life according to the Spirit, the ministerial priesthood is at the service of the common priesthood.

---

[37] Ex 19:6.
[38] Is 61:6.
[39] CCC ¶ 1539.
[40] CCC ¶ 1544.

The ministerial priesthood is a means by which Christ unceasingly builds up and leads His Church."[41]

Father Bob

This might be a good time to introduce you to Father Bob, our parish pastor. Reverend Robert M. Gillelan, Jr. is not only the pastor of our little mission chapel, Our Lady of Fatima in Jonestown, PA, he is also the pastor of our "mother" parish, The Annunciation of the Blessed Virgin Mary (St. Mary's) in Lebanon, PA. The Fatima Chapel is attached financially and organizationally to St. Mary's.

Fr. Bob was ordained a priest for the Diocese of Harrisburg, PA in 1989 by Bishop William Keeler. He has been pastor of several parishes within the Diocese of Harrisburg in addition to being elected to the position of Diocesan Administrator by the College of Consultors of the Diocese of Harrisburg in 2013. As the Diocesan Administrator, it was Fr. Bob's responsibility to help transition the diocese to the era of a new Bishop. The Diocesan Administrator is not the bishop but performs many of the administrative duties of the bishop until a new one is installed. The parish of St. Mary's and the Fatima Chapel are most fortunate to have Fr. Bob as our pastoral leader.

So, what does Fr. Bob have to do with this book? Well, he is a priest, which means he has been ordained through the Sacrament of Holy Orders. Coincidentally, he plays golf, but the real reason he is in this book is because many of the biblical lessons related here are taken, in part, from his Sunday homilies. In fact, it may have been the tenor, or character, of his homilies, that helped me connect the sacraments to the game of golf. The Holy Spirit, no doubt, had a hand in it too.

The Golf Professional in Scripture

Of course, the golf professional is in Scripture too, right? We've already established Adam as the first golf professional, so the origins of the golf professional go way, way back. And, let's not forget the tribe of Levi being set apart for the priesthood. As it relates to following instructions and the consequences of not following

---

[41] CCC ¶ 1547.

instructions, Scripture is abundantly clear from Genesis to Revelation. This relationship between instruction and noncompliance applies directly to the golf professional as well.

For example, in Genesis, God makes a covenant with Abraham. "I am God Almighty; walk before me, and be blameless. And I will make my covenant between me and you, and will multiply you exceedingly."[42] God told Abraham what would happen if he kept the covenant. "I will make you exceedingly fruitful, and I will make nations of you, and kings shall come forth from you."[43] God did put some conditions on this covenant. Faith was God's primary condition, but He also required another one: "You shall be circumcised in the flesh of your foreskins, and it shall be a sign of the covenant between me and you."[44] Abraham followed the Lord's instructions, so he was successful in his journey.

All golfers, beginning or advanced in skills, seek the direction, knowledge, and wisdom of the professional. We go into the pro shop looking for answers. A logical question from the professional would be the same question Jesus asked Bartimaeus, "What do you want me to do for you?"[45] "Bartimaeus, a blind beggar, the son of Timaeus, sitting by the roadside."[46] was looking for answers. He wanted his sight. He wanted to reach the goal. He also knew he couldn't do it by himself. His faith saved him, made him well, and he followed Jesus from that point.

The golf professional will generally begin their instruction process from the beginning, especially if you are a beginning golfer. In my experience, my first lesson began with the proper grip, the interlocking fingers grip. There are other, acceptable grips as well. It was essential to begin with the proper grip. After the grip is established, they'll move on to some swing principles such as backswing, swing plane, weight shift, arm movements, etc. My instructor had me begin swinging with a 7-iron. The 7-iron is traditionally one of the most forgiving clubs and a good midpoint iron, between the wedges and the longer clubs, and generally easier

---

[42] Gn 17:1-2.
[43] Gn 17:6.
[44] Gn 17:11.
[45] Mk 11:51.
[46] Mk 11:46.

to learn the swing.

So, as we consider the importance of the golf professional in our journey toward the goal of getting the ball into the hole, we can see the importance of these instructions and applying the lessons learned. Our chances of achieving success in golf are very significantly related to the amount of time and energy we expend in the learning and development process.

The same is true for our spiritual salvation. The more we learn about our faith, and apply the lessons learned, the more we can participate in the free gift of God's grace. Wait, what? How do we participate in God's grace? Remember, in the previous chapter, we established that obedience to God is essential to our salvation and even our good works are possible, only by the grace of God. We participate in God's grace by obedience. Obedience, and Love, are the theme of Scripture. The Beatitudes illustrate this theme perfectly.

The Beatitudes

Consider the lessons of the Sermon on the Mount in Matthew's Gospel. Jesus, the Supreme golf professional, "opened His mouth and taught them, saying:

Blessed are the poor in spirit, for theirs is the kingdom of heaven.
Blessed are those who mourn, for they shall be comforted.
Blessed are the meek, for they shall inherit the earth.
Blessed are those who hunger and thirst for righteousness, for they shall be satisfied.
Blessed are the merciful, for they shall obtain mercy.
Blessed are the pure in heart, for they shall see God.
Blessed are the peacemakers, for they shall be called sons of God.
Blessed are those who are persecuted for righteousness' sake, for theirs is the kingdom of heaven.
Blessed are you when men revile you and persecute you and utter all kinds of evil against you falsely on my account.
Rejoice and be glad, for your reward is great in heaven."[47]

Jesus taught us these so that if applied in our daily lives, we could more fully participate in the grace of God.

If we relate the Beatitudes to the game of golf, the list might read something like this:

---

[47] Mt 5:2-12.

1. Maintain a good grip and you will be fundamentally sound.
2. Maintain a shoulder width stance and you will have perfect balance.
3. Keep your eyes on the ball and your contact will be pure.
4. Maintain good ball position and your swing will be efficient.
5. Keep your leading arm straight and you will have a consistent swing plane.
6. Maintain an inside-out swing and you will never slice.
7. Execute good hip and body rotation and you will ensure good weight shift.
8. Maintain proper tempo and speed and you will have consistent power and distance.
9. Maintain a good pendulum motion and your putting will be true. Rejoice and be glad, for your reward will be a hole-in-one!

So, what if we do everything perfectly? If all our fundamentals are true and our technique is solid, does that guarantee we get the ball into the hole in the least number of strokes? Sadly, no. There are no guarantees. Even if you can execute each and every shot to perfection, there are still variables out of our control: wind, rain, undulating fairways or greens, and even horribly bad bounces. Some of the variables are fair, some are not.

These variables, fair or not, can also be found in our game of life and in Scripture. Consider Matthew's Gospel on the laborers in the vineyard.

"After agreeing with the laborers for a denarius a day, he sent them into his vineyard. And going out about the third hour, he saw others standing idle in the marketplace, and to them, he said, 'You go into the vineyard, and whatever is right I will give you.' So they went. Going out again about the sixth hour and the ninth hour, he did the same. And about the eleventh hour, he went out and found others standing, and he said to them, 'Why do you stand here idle all day? They said to him, 'Because no one has hired us.' He said to them, 'You go into the vineyard too.' And when evening came, the owner of the vineyard said to his steward, 'Call the laborers and pay them their wages, beginning with the last, up to the first.'[48]

By now, you know the rest of the story. The steward paid each

---

[48] Mt 20:2-8.

laborer a denarius, the agreed wage, regardless of the hours worked in the vineyard. The laborers who worked all day grumbled because they thought they should have received more than the laborers who only worked for an hour.

Golf is so like this parable, isn't it? One golfer can seemingly work endlessly on technique and practice—hours and hours of practice—and perhaps not realize the benefits of "success" while another golfer might practice significantly less but see more benefits. There are no guarantees, but the good news is that the more you practice, the better your chances of success.

A similar example of "no guarantees" from Scripture can be found in the story of the good thief at Christ's crucifixion. The good thief wasn't always good, right? From all biblical accounts, this man was a scoundrel, but he was saved by a faith that his bad thief counterpart did not have. The grace of God that saved this man was free, but we can all agree that in order to participate in this saving grace, the good thief did something, the bad thief did nothing. The story of the good thief drives home the point that we cannot earn our way to Heaven, but it doesn't deny our ability, and perhaps even our requirement, to participate in the grace of God.

Did You Know?

When we profess our faith in the Nicene Creed, we proclaim that we "believe in one, holy, catholic and *apostolic* Church."[49] Nothing says apostolic quite like the Sacrament of Holy Orders. The Catechism states, "Holy Orders is the sacrament through which the mission entrusted by Christ to his apostles continues to be exercised in the Church until the end of time: thus, it is the sacrament of apostolic ministry. Since the sacrament of Holy Orders is the sacrament of the apostolic ministry, it is for the bishops as the successors of the apostles to hand on the "'gift of the Spirit,' the 'apostolic line.'"[50]

Did you know that every Bishop, Priest, and Deacon, by virtue of being validly ordained by a previously validly ordained Bishop, can trace their spiritual lineage back 2,000 years directly to one of the Twelve Apostles? Now, that's what I call true ancestry!

---

[49] CCC The Creed, Pg 63.
[50] CCC ¶ 1536, 1576.

FOUR
On the Tee

(Confirmation)

As we approach the first tee box, we are already members of the club, right? What have we done since our membership began? Well, we probably purchased a great set of golf clubs, we have tees, maybe a glove, and several balls. We should have a good pair of golf shoes and, no doubt, an attractive golf outfit. We have very likely taken lessons from a pro (or others with or without teaching authority), and before we actually approach the first tee, we have probably hit a bucket of balls to get warmed up and ready to play.

Now it is time to "confirm" our commitment and realize the promise of our membership. For me, the Sacrament of Confirmation has always been more of a mystery than the others. Its purpose was less apparent. While some of the Catholic Rites, the Byzantine for example, confer the sacrament at a young age, the Roman Rite does so at an older age, typically during middle school or junior high. Confirmation begins to come into focus and is made more understandable when viewed through the words of the Catechism:

"It must be explained to the faithful that the reception of the sacrament of Confirmation is necessary for the completion of baptismal grace. For "by the sacrament of Confirmation, [the baptized] are more perfectly bound to the Church and are enriched with a special strength of the Holy Spirit. Hence, they are, as true witnesses of Christ, more strictly obliged to spread and defend the faith by word and deed."[51]

Let me repeat for emphasis: Confirmation is necessary *for the completion of baptismal grace.*

---

[51] CCC ¶ 1285.

Whether or not you are baptized as an infant, an adult, or somewhere in between, we all must take our initial promise and commitment to God (Baptism) and become true witnesses of Jesus.

As it relates to golf, "learning" how to play the game—obtaining proper equipment and relentless practice—correlates directly to Confirmation because, by being active in our quest to fulfill our promises of membership in the club, the process of receiving the graces of Confirmation assists our quest to fulfill our Baptismal promises and ensures our being "enriched with a special strength of the Holy Spirit."[52]

Confirmation, through Jesus Christ, marks us as Christians. Consider the effects of Confirmation as stated in the Catechism:[53]

- It roots us more deeply in the divine filiation which makes us cry, "Abba! Father!"
- It unites us more firmly to Christ
- It increases the gifts of the Holy Spirit in us
- It renders our bond with the Church more perfect
- It gives us a special strength of the Holy Spirit to spread and defend the faith by word and action as true witnesses of Christ, to confess the name of Christ boldly, and never to be ashamed of the Cross

When we apply the effects of Confirmation to the game of golf, we can also see how the "light bulb" goes on the more we expand our instruction and practice. The search for perfection in the game of golf is as intense as it is in life. In life, we strive to "be perfect as your heavenly Father is perfect."[54] We strive to do this by obeying the Commandments and living the Gospel. In golf, we also strive for perfection through means of instruction, and lots of practice. We can no sooner master the understanding of any mystery of God more than we can master the game of golf, but we are constantly encouraged by our faith, hope, and love of both. We endure many ups and downs throughout. Both require huge amounts of faith. Fr. Richard Simon from Relevant Radio likes to say, "Faith equals

---

[52] CCC ¶ 1285.
[53] CCC ¶ 1303.
[54] Mt 5:48

Trust."[55] We place tremendous amounts of trust in our inspired mentors, be they clergy or golf professionals. Our efforts are often rewarded. If we persevere in practice and preparation, we DO execute good shots. We may even be able to pull off several pars or better within each round. At the very least, we'll crush a drive or make a difficult putt.

In the face of tribulation and great difficulty, Jesus said, "But he who endures to the end will be saved."[56] In His Sermon on the Mount, he said, "Rejoice and be glad, for your reward is great in heaven."[57] Clearly, our eventual successes are tied directly to our efforts. I love Deacon Doug Cook's paraphrase of Mt 5:12, "He didn't say it would be easy, but He promised it would be worth it"[58]

"He didn't say it would be easy…" is very appropriately applied to golf, isn't it? One of the more frustrating aspects of golf is the seeming lack of consistency in our results. How come we can't hit a 7-iron the same every time? Chipping and putting seem like the easiest parts of the game, why do we chunk chips and hammer putts off the green? Why is my new nickname "3-putt Chuck"?

3-Putt Chuck in Scripture

I began playing the game of golf when I was a senior in high school. It actually began in my Government class on Civics. Mr. Skillman, God rest his soul, was our instructor. He was a bit of an outlier in his teaching methods. The first semester of the class was actual Civics, and the second half was independent study. Even though I was a senior, I was way too immature to handle independent study. I needed firm direction. I wasn't capable of picking a topic and learning all on my own. I completed the first semester nicely. It was very structured, to my liking, and I learned all about how our government works. In the independent study semester, we were tasked with finding our own area of study. My brain was empty. I couldn't come up with anything. Mr. Skillman tried to jar something loose in my brain so that I wouldn't fail the class. I remember him asking me what I did for enjoyment. I

[55] Father Richard Simon. Relevant Radio, Podcast.
[56] Mt 24:13.
[57] Mt 5:12.
[58] Deacon Doug Cook, Executive Director. Orange County California Cursillo.

immediately shared that I had just recently played a round of golf for the first time, and I really enjoyed it. He said, "Make golf your independent study." I said, "Whoa! What a great idea." My golf "career" was officially started.

I remember going to the library and checking out a book on how to play golf. I believe it was written by Ben Hogan, but I can't remember the name of the book. What I remember are the photos. It had a series of progressive photos of Ben Hogan's swing. There was a different photo on each page, and when you flipped through the pages, you would see his entire swing in motion, as if it were a slow-motion replay. Soon, I would join my buddies for more rounds of golf, and I quickly fell in love with the game. That was 53 years ago.

So, for the past half-century, I've been toiling around with this game. Mostly, I've relied on my exceptional physical strength. It was not uncommon for me to swing as hard as I could and try to hit it as far as I could. This, of course, is not the way to master the game of golf. I could very easily draw parallels between my approach to golf and the youthful approach to my faith, more slog than splash and lots of idleness. I was in this state of idleness until I retired, then I began applying the principles behind the Sacrament of Confirmation to my golf. I looked for instruction and guidance. I had already been "baptized" into the golfing community, and now I needed to put into practice the "graces" of my instruction and guidance so that I could complete the "baptismal promises" of golf.

Where does "3-Putt Chuck" come from? Well, that's actually a nickname I gave myself. I would like to report that after more than 50 years of playing golf, I have become a scratch golfer. Sadly, I cannot. I have improved markedly, but my chipping and putting are woefully poor. In a recent round, I three putted eight holes. Indeed, *He didn't say it would be easy, but He promised it would be worth it!*

As a result of my poor showing on the greens, I've redoubled my efforts to improve my putting. I've also looked to Matthew's Gospel for inspiration and instruction: "Teacher, what good deed must I do to have eternal life? And He said to him, why do you ask me about what is good? One, there is who is good. If you would enter life, keep the commandments.'[59] "The young man said to him, 'All of these I have observed; what do I still lack?' Jesus said to him, 'If you would be perfect, go, sell what you possess and give to the poor, and you will have treasure in heaven, and come follow me.'"[60] So, as this relates to golf, it is great advice. I feel like I've followed instructions and attempted to apply my practice to live action on the course, but I'm positive I haven't given everything to be a good putter. I need to "sell" my pride and the false sense of golfing worth and follow the true path to good putting.

Where's My Pentecost?

Pentecost is often called the birthday of the Apostolic Church. Even though this feast has its origins in the Old Testament, it was a celebration of the spring harvest, it is now one of the most revered feasts of the Christian Church. "On several occasions Christ promised this outpouring of the Spirit, a promise which he fulfilled first on Easter Sunday and then more strikingly at Pentecost."[61] It was at this Pentecost that the Holy Spirit descended on them. "And they were all filled with the Holy Spirit and began to speak in other tongues, as the Spirit gave them utterance."[62]

Remember when Jesus was with the Apostles during his three-year public ministry, Jesus had to gently rebuke them repeatedly for not understanding His message. It happened several times. James and John and their mother were rebuked when they came to Jesus and asked that they be granted seats next to Jesus in heaven, "one at your right hand and one at your left in your glory. But Jesus said to them, 'You do not know what you are asking.'"[63]

Peter received the brunt of these gentle rebukes. When Peter tried to walk on water, "but when he saw the wind, he was afraid, and beginning to sink he cried out, 'Lord, save me.' Jesus immediately reached out his hand and caught him, saying to him, 'O you of little faith, why did you doubt?'"[64]

---

[59] Mt 19:16-17.
[60] Mt 19:20-21.
[61] CCC ¶ 1287.

[62] Acts 2:4.
[63] Mk 10:37-38.
[64] Mt 14:30-33.

Peter was rebuked again, this time right after Peter proclaimed Jesus to be Christ. "And he (Jesus) began to teach them that the Son of man must suffer many things… and be killed, and after three days rise again… And Peter took him and began to rebuke him. But turning and seeing his disciples, he rebuked Peter, and said, 'Get behind me, Satan! For you are not on the side of God, but of men.'"[65] In fact, Jesus tried to tell the disciples on at least three occasions that he would be killed, and after three days, he would rise. They just didn't get it.

But, on Pentecost, they *did* get it. They had their "aha" moments big time. They understood everything. This applies to golf too. We joined the club and received some preliminary instruction and guidance (Baptism), but it is not until we've had extensive training and formation that we truly get it. That's Confirmation! Confirmation is associated with Pentecost because it is in and through the Sacrament of Confirmation that we all *get* it.

So, where is your Pentecost in golf? Well, I would argue that every time you absolutely crush a drive straight down the middle of the fairway, or when you smack a tee shot on a par 3 and it rolls right into the hole, you experience that "I know exactly what I did" feeling. You have experienced Pentecost, the same Pentecost the disciples experienced.

Confirmation provides the tools we need to be true apostolic witnesses. When we get dressed up in our terrific golf attire, load up our clubs, warm up, and head to the first tee, are we not true witnesses to the game of golf?

---

[65] Mk 8:31-33.

Did You Know?

Do you remember the Confirmation "slap?" This custom has not really been in use since the early 1970s, although it is not prohibited. The "slap" was never an essential element of the sacrament. (Remember that each sacrament needs Form-Matter-Intent to be valid.) The Form for Confirmation is the bishop's prayer, the Matter is the Sacred Chrism (oil) and laying on of hands, and the Intent is, of course, the intention to be confirmed. Traditionally, "the slight slap on the cheek by the bishop signifies that the confirmed will face the buffetings of the world for the sake of Christ Jesus and the proclamation of the good news of his Crucifixion and Resurrection, the *kerygma*, but that they have been made firm in the faith, hope, and love of Christ by this sacrament."[66]

According to Archbishop Wilton D. Gregory, "In reality, that slap was a variation of the sign of peace that the bishop now gives to each candidate after confirming him or her. Like the gentle touch of the hand that parents might give to a sleeping child, it was a sign of affection and tenderness rather than an expression of "tough love." However, the gesture did manage to become one of the most memorable parts of the ceremony of Confirmation, lasting decades in the memories of Catholics long after it disappeared from the actual ritual. Would that other ritual gestures have such a long life in the minds and hearts of the faithful!"[67]

---

[66] Fr. Philip-Michael Tangorra. St. Paul Center Digital Library.

[67] Archbishop Wilton D. Gregory, *Commentary. Reflections on yesteryear's Confirmation "slap",* (Aug. 1, 2013).

FIVE
Food for the Journey

(The Eucharist)

We have completed our lessons, received valuable guidance, prepared ourselves thoroughly, and are now ready to approach the first tee box with confidence. Before we put a tee into the ground, we must stop at the Grill, right? If we have an early morning tee time, we might want to begin with a cup of coffee, maybe a donut or bagel. If we need something a little more potent, we might start with a Bloody Mary or a Transfusion. If we are beginning a little later, say mid-morning or even an afternoon tee time, we might begin with a sandwich, soda or beer, and perhaps some peanut butter crackers.

As we transition from the lessons learned and begin to apply these lessons on the golf course, we recall the symbolism found in every Holy Mass. First, we hear and learn from the Word of God as we listen to Old and New Testament readings, the Psalms, and the Gospel. Then, we get nourished by God through the Eucharist—indeed, Food for the journey!

The Scriptures mention food and sustenance frequently. When we speak of the Eucharist, symbolism is ever present, but symbolism often takes a back seat to God's actual words.

Bishop Barron, in his speech to the National Eucharistic Congress (Indianapolis), quoted a famous Catholic apologist, Bishop Ronald Knox, saying (paraphrasing), "Almost all of Jesus Christ's commands have been dishonored or disregarded. Commands like; Love your enemies, bless those that curse you, don't judge, etc. We habitually disregard these commands, but over the years, this one command we have consistently obeyed: "Do this in remembrance of Me."[68] "Somehow, we know we must follow that command," says Bishop Barron.

The bishop had another striking point. When God said, "Let there be light",[69] through faith and our knowledge of scripture, and as it says in Genesis, *"And it was so."*[70] We have come to know that what God says...IS! When Jesus said, "Do this in remembrance of Me."[71], and because we know Jesus is not just one prophet among many prophets, he is God from God, Light from Light. We know Jesus is God; therefore, "What Jesus says... IS! This is the basic theology of the Church, the theology of the Real Presence."[72] *"And it was so."*[73]

In the Bread of Life discourse (John Chapter 6) Jesus explicitly states, several times, eat My flesh, drink My blood. "Truly, truly, I say to you, unless you eat the flesh of the Son of Man and drink his blood, you have no life in you... for My flesh is food indeed, and My blood is drink indeed."[74] What Jesus says... IS!

Sustenance is an appropriate part of this discussion, especially as we continue on our journey toward the goal. The Grill provides us with sustenance for our journey through 18 holes. It is significant to note that our food for the journey, whether it be from the Grill or God himself, is intended for our sustenance. It is not necessarily meant to take away our afflictions or suffering. The Eucharist is the Body, Blood, Soul, and Divinity of Jesus Christ. It is our spiritual food as well. It sustains us spiritually while we are on this earth. The Eucharist is not some magical food from the fountain of youth. It sustains us spiritually and keeps us nourished for the journey ahead.

Sustenance in Scripture

Where else do we witness God's power of sustenance? When Moses led the Israelites through the desert, God didn't shorten the journey or take away the suffering—it still took them forty long years to get to the Promised Land—but He did sustain them with

---

[68] Lk 22:19.
[69] Gn 1:3.
[70] Gn 1:11.
[71] Lk 22:19.
[72] Bishop Barren speech at National Eucharistic Congress, Indianapolis 2024.
[73] Gn1:11.
[74] Jn 6:53-55.

food and drink: manna from heaven and water from the rock. "When the sons of Israel saw it, they said to one another, 'What is it?' And Moses said to them, 'It is the bread which the LORD has given you to eat.'"[75]

In 1st Kings, Elijah was being pursued by Jezebel. Elijah, tired, weary and having enough of the running, "came and sat down under a broom tree; and he asked the LORD that he might die…. and he lay down and slept under a broom tree."[76] God had other plans for Elijah, so when he woke, "there was at his head a cake baked on hot stones and a jar of water."[77] God, through his angel, repeated this a second time, saying, "Arise and eat, else the journey will be too great for you."[78] God didn't take away his affliction or suffering, He sustained him. This is what the Eucharist does for us today.

We find this also in the New Testament. Jesus taught them first (The Sermon on the Mount), and then He fed them. In Mark's Gospel, "As He landed, He saw a great throng, and He had compassion on them, because they were like sheep without a shepherd; and He began to teach them many things."[79] Soon after this, He fed them. "Jesus said, 'Make the people sit down.' Now there was much grass in the place; so, the men sat down, in number about five thousand. Jesus then took the loaves, and when he had given thanks, he distributed them to those who were seated; and so also the fish, as much as they wanted."[80]

In his sermon on this subject, Fr. Bob adds that we should not let the symbolism of Jesus —teaching—The Liturgy of the Word—then feeding—The Liturgy of the Eucharist—escape us when pondering the connection to the Holy Mass.

The Catechism states, "The Eucharist is the source and summit of the Christian life. The other sacraments, and indeed all ecclesiastical ministries and works of the apostolate, are bound up with the Eucharist and are oriented toward it."[81]

---

[75] Ex 16:15.
[76] 1Kgs 19:4-5.
[77] 1Kgs 19:6.
[78] 1Kgs 19:7.
[79] Mk: 6:34.
[80] Jn 6:10-11.
[81] CCC ¶ 1324.

The Eucharist has been given several different names. "*Eucharist*, because it is an action of thanksgiving to God.[82] *The Lord's Supper*, because of its connection with the supper which the Lord took with his disciples on the eve of his Passion and because it anticipates the wedding feast of the Lamb in the heavenly Jerusalem. *The Breaking of Bread*, because Jesus used this rite, part of a Jewish meal, when as master of the table he blessed and distributed the bread, above all at the Last Supper."[83] One of my all-time favorites in Scripture is the Gospel story of the Road to Emmaus. "He took the bread and blessed and broke it, and gave it to them. And their eyes were opened, and they recognized him."[84]

The Catechism further summarizes the Eucharist as follows: "We must therefore consider the Eucharist as thanksgiving and praise to the *Father*; the sacrificial memorial of *Christ* and his Body; the presence of Christ by the power of his word and of his *Spirit*."[85] Father Mike Schmitz, adds to this his own summation, "The heart of religion is worship, the heart of worship is sacrifice."[86]

And a final thought on the Real Presence, to go along with Bishop Barren's statements on the subject, is an argument put forth by St. Robert Bellarmine, "If Christ said, 'he who eats my flesh and drinks my blood has eternal life.' Who are we to contradict the Son of God?"[87]

Eucharistic Miracles

Eucharistic miracles have been reported many times since the time of Jesus. I would encourage everyone to look them up. Read about them. Some of these reported miracles have been officially recognized by the Church, but many have not. Most are compelling.

I have my own minor Eucharistic miracle moment.

Many years ago, while living in southern California, I attended a Cursillo weekend. Cursillistas, as we are called, do not describe

---

[82] CCC ¶ 1328.

[83] CCC ¶ 1329.

[84] Lk 24:30-31.

[85] CCC ¶ 1358.

[86] Fr. Mike Schmitz, *Catechism in a Year* podcast, *Day 185*, (Ascension Press).

[87] Fr. John A. Hardon, S.J., *Great Catholic Books Newsletter. Volume I, Number 9.* Jn 6:54.

these weekend events as retreats but rather as a movement. Briefly, the Cursillo movement is a three-day weekend that includes fifteen talks—Rollos (meaning short courses). The main goal is to encourage participants to apply what they've learned in the real world, referred to as the fourth day.

One of the high points of the weekend, and there were many, was the availability to go to Eucharistic Adoration. The Adoration Chapel at the Divine Word Retreat Center in Riverside, CA is an awesome place for Adoration. It is such a reverent and beautiful setting for visiting with Jesus. We were able and encouraged to visit with Jesus in the Blessed Sacrament as often as we wanted, but during the weekend *rollos*, each table (De Curia) was specifically scheduled for a period of Adoration as a group. Our table consisted of three participants and two table leaders, Wade and David.

I do have some history with Eucharistic Adoration. When I was grade school and high school age, I would attend nocturnal Adoration with my dad. As I mentioned, my dad was a member of The Holy Name Society, and one of their primary ministries was facilitating monthly adoration in our parish chapel. This was done on the first Friday of every month, from 7 p.m. Friday night to 7 a.m. Saturday morning. Members of this group would volunteer to take one hour and it rotated every month, so we all had a turn at each hour. At first, it was very cool, but when I was in high school, it was not as cool, especially when we were assigned the early morning hours. But, looking back, I have only fond memories of these First Friday Adorations with Jesus and my Dad.

So, at the Cursillo, our table group was kneeling right up next to the altar and the Blessed Sacrament, and we were allowed to touch the monstrance, something I had never done before—actually, I didn't think it was allowed. As we knelt, our team leaders, Wade and David, prayed for us and provided us with good examples of prayers to offer before Jesus, then invited each of us to pray aloud too. I went first, and I remember praying for our daughter Tarah, the safe delivery of her expectant baby, that the doctors would use all of their skills and training to allow for a safe delivery when the baby was ready to come into the world, and for safe travels for Carolyn as she had a flight from LAX to Harrisburg, PA to assist our daughter.

Whenever I attended an Adoration in the past, I always looked intently at the large Host to see if I could see the face of Jesus. This time was no different. I looked directly at the consecrated Host. In just a couple of minutes, I saw Him! Or at least I saw a bearded man with deep-set eyes. Even though I had never seen this image before, I thought for sure this was Jesus. I wanted to sear this image into my memory, so I stared intently and didn't want to move my eyes away and lose it. It wasn't too long, but long enough, that His image disappeared. I don't remember being disappointed. I was happy I was able to see Him as an image and likeness, even for a short moment. I looked away for a few seconds. When I looked back at the Host to see if I could find Him again, I didn't see Him. Instead, I saw my mother. It was a perfect likeness of her just as I've seen her in many photos. Of course, I have always loved my mother, but I wasn't particularly thinking of her at the time. Her image just appeared on the Host in the same way that Jesus appeared, both were facing toward my right. She, too, disappeared after a few moments.

Again, I wasn't disappointed she left, but I was extremely happy I saw her for even a short moment. A few seconds passed, then I thought of my Dad. Of course, I've always loved my Dad, too. I tried intently to see if his image would appear. It did not. I was a bit disappointed, and I was left wondering what all of this meant. Not too long after this, our Adoration hour ended, and we returned to our *Rollos* session. I remember feeling energized and uplifted, but after the Cursillo weekend was completed, it got better.

On that Monday, literally the fourth day, I began writing down my memory of the adoration experience. That evening, I browsed through the pamphlets in my *Palanca* bag, looking for bedtime reading.

The *Palanca* bag (Spanish for spiritual lever) is another amazing aspect of Cursillo. I would describe it as a bag full of Valentine's Day cards. The bag consisted of hundreds of personal letters written by my brothers and sisters in Christ, offering prayers, sacrifices, and encouragement for me. People from all over the world who don't even know me are praying for me and offering personal sacrifices: for *me.* It was very emotional reading each letter. I remember my eyes welling up and being a bit misty as I read them.

Also included in the bag were many pamphlets and prayer cards. One particular pamphlet that caught my eye was entitled: *I Thirst. A*

Guided Meditation with Mother Teresa.[88] So I began to scan through the pages. I turned over one page, and on the top was a photo of an oil painting called "Head of Christ" by Rembrandt. As soon as I saw this photo, I just remembered saying to myself, "Whoa!"

The "Head of Christ" was the same exact image I saw in the Eucharistic Host during Adoration, the bearded man with deep set eyes. This, too, was a very emotional moment for me.

Below are the Monstrance and the two images I saw in the Eucharistic Host during Adoration. Food for the journey, indeed. That is the kind of sustenance we need on the golf course.

| Head of Christ by Rembrandt | Monstrance – Blessed Sacrament | My mother – Muriel Gilson |

[88] Fr. Joseph Langford, Missionaries of Charity Fathers, *A Meditation,*(pamphlet), (Our Sunday Visitor, 1986).

Did You Know?

The Council of Trent summarizes the Catholic faith by declaring, "Because Christ our Redeemer said that it was truly his body that he was offering under the species of bread, it has always been the conviction of the Church of God, and this holy Council now declares again, that by the consecration of the bread and wine, there takes place a change of the whole substance of the bread into the substance of the body of Christ our Lord and of the whole substance of the wine into the substance of his blood. This change the holy Catholic Church has fittingly and properly called transubstantiation."[89]

"The Eucharistic presence of Christ begins at the moment of the consecration and endures as long as the Eucharistic species subsist."[90]

Did you know that when we present ourselves and take part in this wonderful sacrament, we are actively participating in the "remembrance," as Jesus had instructed, and, for as long as the Eucharistic species subsist in our body, we are His tabernacle, providing a resting place for God.

---

[89] CCC ¶1376.
[90] CCC ¶ 1377.

SIX
Fairway to Heaven

(Matrimony)

We are members of the club, dressed for success, fresh from our instruction and training, and nourished at the grill—we are ready to tee off.

The first tee shot of every round is always a bit nervy. The tee area around the first hole can be a hub of activity. Many times, there are other groups waiting to tee off or others finishing up their round nearby. It is wise to calm the nerves, relax, and concentrate on what you need to do. If all goes well, you'll hit your tee shot long and straight and find the fairway.

There is no better way to calm the nerves, relax, and concentrate on what we need to do than to golf with a friend, a buddy, or a partner—and many times, your friend, buddy, or partner is the same person—your spouse. Of course, this assumes they are not speaking as you swing.

Rules of Marriage

Matrimony and golf literally go hand-in-hand. Many years ago, I had read something about the three rules of marriage. I don't know who to attribute these rules to, so apologies for that. Just know, I didn't originate them:

1. Marriage is forever
2. Have lots of children
3. Help each other get to Heaven

Rule 1: Marriage is forever

The Catechism describes Marriage nicely: "The matrimonial covenant, by which a man and a woman establish between themselves a partnership of the whole life, is by its nature ordered toward the good of the spouses and the procreation and education of offspring; this covenant between baptized persons has been raised by Christ the Lord to the dignity of a sacrament."[91]

Amazingly, the institution of marriage itself is well over 4,000 years old. The Catechism goes on to say, "Sacred Scripture begins with the creation of man and woman in the image and likeness of God and concludes with a vision of 'the wedding feast of the Lamb.'"[92] When Jesus arrived on the scene, He "refreshed" the institution by reminding us that its original intent hadn't changed. Jesus and the New Testament authors provided for us—through the Sacrament of Matrimony—the "rules of the road," so to speak.

In a recent Mass, the Old Testament reading, the Gospel reading, and the homily were about Marriage and its divine origin. The Old Testament reading was from Genesis 2:18-24, "The two of them become one flesh." The commentary accompanying this reading, as published by Universalis, is equally striking and worthy of its full content as presented:

"By giving the animals their names, the Man is taking part in their creation. Made in the image of God, the Man's task is to promote God's work and foster creation and foster life, just as God himself does. The creation of human beings is the climax of creation, which means that human beings have a responsibility towards the rest of creation. The warm ideal relationship between God and the Man before the Fall is particularly touching. God's care for the Man, putting him to sleep before the surgical operation and himself sewing up the wound is delightful. So is God's careful molding of the Woman and the presentation of his handiwork to the Man. It is important to see that there is no unevenness between the sexes, each is personally molded by God. Their welcome for each other is the author's pictorial way of showing that the bonding between them in marriage is a divine institution."[93]

In the Gospel reading, Jesus, when tested by the Pharisees, confirms (He even quotes the Genesis reading) and makes clear the intentions of God the Father and the divine institution of Marriage.

---

[91] CCC ¶ 1601.

[92] CCC ¶ 1602.

[93] Readings at Mass, *27th Sunday in Ordinary Time,* (Universalis Publishing Limited, Oct. 6, 2024).

Jesus summarizes this by saying, "What therefore God has joined together, let not man put asunder."[94] This attests to the permanent nature of Marriage.

Just a quick note about annulments of marriage. Sadly, many marriages are ended before the natural death of one of the spouses. There is a good bit of confusion surrounding this subject. It is not my intent to clear up the confusion but only to suggest that seemingly, not all marriages last forever. The Church uses the annulment process to determine if a valid marriage ever existed in the first place. The sacrament of Matrimony requires, as the Catechism states, that the couple must "freely express their consent."[95] "If this freedom is lacking the marriage is invalid."[96] The Catechism goes on to say, "For this reason (or for other reasons that render the marriage null and void) the Church, after an examination of the situation by the competent ecclesiastical tribunal, can declare the nullity of a marriage, i.e., that the marriage never existed."[97] There are many things that make up the essentials for a valid marriage, free consent, no impedance of natural law, etc.

Fr. Mike, in his Catechism-in-a-Year podcast, used a great analogy describing the essentials of a valid marriage, chocolate chips![98] When baking chocolate chip cookies, there are several ingredients that make up the recipe, flour, sugar, milk, eggs, etc. However, there is one essential ingredient that must be in every chocolate chip cookie: chocolate chips.

So, on the surface, annulments may not seem to factor into a golf game, but my brother-in-law, Steve, completed his own process of golf annulment. After years of toil, he determined he lacked the "chocolate chips" required for this game. There are rumors that his clubs can be found at the bottom of Lake Nottley. A bit whimsical, but it makes the point.

Enough about annulments.

---

[94] Mk 10:9.
[95] CCC ¶ 1625.
[96] CCC ¶ 1628.
[97] CCC ¶ 1629.
[98] Fr. Mike Schmitz, *Catechism in a Year. Podcast, Day 222*, (Ascension Press).

Rule 2: Have lots of children

Well, it's hard to put a number on "lots." When marriage vows are exchanged, the mutual consent that binds the partners to each other finds fulfillment in the two "becoming one flesh."[99] It is literally fulfilled when children become the fruit of this consent. The Catechism and Scripture explain it this way, "And this love (Marriage) which God blesses is intended to be fruitful and to be realized in the common work of watching over creation: And God blessed them, and God said to them: 'Be fruitful and multiply, and fill the earth.'"[100] Granted, the idea of having lots of children isn't so much related to the game of golf, but the idea of commitment and discipline, as it relates to child-rearing is. The promises, commitments, and responsibilities discussed in Baptism are as applicable to raising children as they are to golf.

The Catechism quotes *Gaudium et spes:*

"Children are the supreme gift of marriage and contribute greatly to the good of the parents themselves… wishing to associate them in a special way in his own creative work… hence, true married love and the whole structure of family life which results from it, without diminishment of the other ends of marriage, are directed to disposing the spouses to cooperate valiantly with the love of the Creator and Savior, who through them will increase and enrich his family from day to day."[101]

"The fruitfulness of conjugal love extends to the fruits of the moral, spiritual, and supernatural life that parents hand on to their children by education. Parents are the principal and first educators of their children."[102]

Education involves discipline. Discipline involves perseverance and obedience—both find their origins in Scripture—and both are equally applicable to golf and our journey toward the goal. Discipline is training to obey the rules or a code of behavior, and it is something that parents, and golfers, with or without children, must have and must do. Yes, it involves punishment to correct disobedience. The disciplinary process, imbedded within the

---

[99] Gn 2:24.
[100] CCC ¶ 1604. Gn 1:28.
[101] GS 50 § 1.CCC ¶ 1652.
[102] CCC ¶ 1653.

parent's educational methods, can vary widely. My parents were of the old-school method. They taught me and my siblings the importance of obedience. It is worth mentioning that this old-school method is not entirely what today's young parents believe it to be. When we discuss this subject around the kitchen table or living room, our now-grown kids think we were slap-happy, rump-beating parents. To set the record straight, we were not slap-happy, rump-beating parents, but we did have the "proverbial disciplinary toolbox," and we used all the tools available.

I like to compare our method to the progressive disciplinary process used in many businesses. When an employee breaks the work rules they are given a verbal warning. Further non-compliance results in a progressive path that ultimately leads to termination, or better yet, compliance. The verbal warning is the key. If done effectively, the need for further action is eliminated or diminished dramatically. Of course, children cannot be terminated in the same sense as an employee, but the initial verbal warning is still the key.

Once the verbal warning is issued, it is game on, challenge accepted. The line has been drawn. The parent(s) and the child have entered into a mutual agreement, essentially a verbal contract. What follows the verbal warning depends entirely on the parties involved. Will the parents achieve the compliance (obedience) they're looking for? Will the children obey? It's been my experience that this first verbal agreement is a total failure. None of the parties to the agreement comply with any of their own commitments. The child doesn't behave, and the parent(s) don't follow up on the promised consequences. If only one party had been non-compliant, usually the child, then a valuable lesson would have been learned. This lesson learned will carry forward and diminish the need for further action.

When both the child and parent(s) are non-compliant, a valuable lesson is still learned, but it's not the lesson you really wanted to be taught. The lesson learned, obviously, is that the child knows the verbal warning is meaningless. This is bad, precisely because it guarantees further action will be necessary. Sometimes the action will evolve into a progressive process with increasing tension, including raised voices, lost tempers, more threats of punishment, or worse.

In the Introduction to this book, I mentioned that my father was really good at this discipline game. I don't recall that he was ever non-compliant with any of the "verbal contracts" we had between us.

Naturally, as kids, we wouldn't comply with the first one, but we quickly learned that it was not wise to do so. There was no option for "three strikes and you're out," or the "1-2-3" counting method. These methods were horribly flawed from the outset. They were essentially permissions for both parties not to comply. The child soon learned that warning numbers one and two meant absolutely nothing. Eventually warning number three would also be meaningless. The parent(s) would learn that they could effectively defer or avoid the entire disciplinary process altogether. The child would learn to do something cute or funny, the parent(s) would melt with joy—so much for discipline—until the next episode of misbehavior.

When I recall my formative years, I don't recall the spankings or my hands being slapped, both happened, as much as I remembered there would be consequences for my non-compliant behavior. The spankings and hand slaps were few and far between, but the lessons lived on.

One more thing. Carolyn and I mimicked our parent's methods, with the way we raised our own children. We were always on the same page of the disciplinary playbook. Sometimes discipline isn't about corrections or punishments, but instead, it resembles strength, an inner strength, and confident authority. Sometimes it's just a matter of exuding that inner strength. A mother's love for a child sometimes looks very different than a father's love for a child. A child is *happiest* when attached to mommy, mommy's shadow. A child feels *safest* when sitting on daddy's lap. Parents are constantly juggling which type of discipline is needed, safe or happy, and how much intensity should be used. It's a process that seems to be an endless challenge, doesn't it?

Rule 3: Help each other get to Heaven

This rule is the one I think of most, as it relates to golf. Of course, there are many reasons for having a golf buddy, fellowship, advice, counseling, and business discussions are but a few. Like Holy Orders, the sacrament of Matrimony "is directed towards the salvation of others; if they contribute as well to personal salvation, it is through service to others that they do so."[103] The Catechism defines this more thoroughly. "This grace proper to the sacrament of Matrimony is intended to perfect the couple's love and to strengthen their indissoluble unity. By this grace, they 'help one another to attain

---

[103] CCC ¶ 1534.

holiness in their married life and in welcoming and educating their children.' Christ is the source of this grace... Christ dwells with them, gives them the strength to take up their crosses and so follow him, to rise again after they have fallen, to forgive one another, to bear one another's burdens, to 'be subject to one another out of reverence for Christ.'"[104]

St. Thomas Aquinas is often attributed with this definition of Love: it means to consistently will and choose the good of the other. Pope Paul VI went a little further in his Encyclical *Gaudian et Spes*:

For this reason, love for God and neighbor is the first and greatest commandment. Sacred Scripture, however, teaches us that the love of God cannot be separated from love of neighbor: "If there is any other commandment, it is summed up in this saying: Thou shalt love thy neighbor as thyself.... Love therefore is the fulfillment of the Law" (Rom. 13:9-10; cf. 1 John 4:20). To men growing daily more dependent on one another, and to a world becoming more unified every day, this truth proves to be of paramount importance.[105]

Bishop Barron summarizes it this way. Love "is the perfection of both willing another's good *and* of the total gift of self."[106] While playing golf, I have often seen examples of "willing the good of the other." I have consistently been on the receiving end of well wishes and sincere hopes that I will hit the ball long and straight. Indeed, it is hard to find golf partners that are anything but encouraging and positive toward the other, unless, of course, there are serious wagers involved.

For another example of help on our journey, let's revisit our blind friend Bartimaeus. Mark writes in his Gospel, "As they came to Jericho; and as He was leaving Jericho with His disciples and a great multitude, Bartimaeus, a blind beggar, was sitting by the roadside."[107] As we know, Jesus was on His *way* to Jerusalem. Emphasis on *way* because in the time of Jesus and shortly thereafter, many Christians identified themselves as followers of Jesus by

---

[104] CCC ¶ 1641-1642.

[105] Pope Paul IV, *Gaudian et Spes*, Dec. 7, 1965.

[106] Dr. Tom Neal, *To Will The Good Of The Other*, (WordonFire.org., Feb. 24, 2014).

[107] Mk 10:46.

claiming they are part of the *Way* or Jesus is the *Way*. If you were a follower of the *Way*, you were considered a Christian. As the story continues, we know that Jesus gives sight to Bartimaeus and says, "Go your way; your faith has made you well."[108] The very next line in the Gospel is the kicker. "And immediately he received his sight and followed Him on the way."[109]

Fr. Bob, in a homily on the Bartimaeus story, asked an interesting question. Bartimaeus followed Jesus on the way. Did Bartimaeus follow Jesus the whole way? Hmmm. To give this a little perspective, Fr. Bob injected a small geography lesson. Jericho was situated near the Dead Sea, one of the lowest elevations on the planet, at nearly 900 feet below sea level. Jerusalem is about 20 miles away, sitting about 3,000 feet above sea level. The road to Jerusalem was said to be fraught with danger in places involving robbers and thugs to go along with the nearly 4,000-foot climb to the city. So, the journey to Jerusalem can be reasonably equated to the dangers we face on our fair*way* to Heaven, and the fairways of the golf course.

We probably won't get robbed or beat up on the golf course, although I was shot at twice on a fairway in California, a story for another day. But traps, water hazards, trees, and knee-deep rough can easily come into play, and interrupt our otherwise beautiful journey on the fairway. Bartimaeus no doubt had many other followers of Jesus to assist him along the *way,* and Scripture is silent on whether or not Bartimaeus made the journey all the way to Jerusalem but with the full commitment of our golf partner, we, too, have the help we need to journey through the fairways of golf , and our fair*way* to Heaven.

---

[108] Mk 10:52
[109] Mk 10:52.

Did You Know?

In all of the sacraments, there are ordinary ministers who confer the sacrament, and there are conferees who receive the sacrament. Usually, the ministers of the sacraments are bishops, priests, or deacons (the main exception being Baptism in the case of necessity).

Did you know in Matrimony, it is the spouses themselves that are the ministers of Matrimony, and the bishops, priests, or deacons are the witnesses? According to the Catechism, "the spouses as ministers of Christ's grace mutually confer upon each other the sacrament of Matrimony by expressing their consent before the Church... the priests (bishops or presbyters) are witnesses to the mutual consent given by the spouses, but for the validity of the sacrament their blessing is also necessary."[110]

---

[110] CCC ¶ 1623.

SEVEN
Water Hazards

(Reconciliation)

We have been Baptized and Confirmed. We have received the wisdom and counsel of Holy Orders. We've been nourished with the Body, Blood, Soul, and Divinity of our Lord Jesus Christ in the Eucharist. So, together with our spouse, arguably the best golf buddy ever, we find ourselves on the fair*way* to Heaven. What could possibly go wrong?

A Slice of Humble Pie

Nothing so forcefully demands a large slice of humble pie quite like being a golfer. Growing in humility might be the true purpose of this game. You're either humbled by the sport, or you will likely be destroyed by it. The game can be horribly frustrating, at the very least. It is a game that is never, ever, really mastered. But, at the lowest level, my level, you can still have reasonably good days. I've had years where I was a solid 30 handicap, scores ranging from mid-90s to 105 or worse. After retiring from my work-a-day world, I played more often and whittled the handicap index down to around a 12 at my best, to an 18 or so, roughly scoring in the low to mid-80s, and maybe dipping into the high 70s on an easy course (and from the senior tees of course). But, I could, and quite often did, follow up a great round, maybe a 12 index, with a horrible round, maybe a 25 or worse. How is that possible, right? And you don't have to wait until your next round to experience the ups and downs of this game. Typically, in a round of 18 holes, a golfer will experience a run of very good holes, followed by some brain-dead garbage holes. It happens all the time… I dare say it happens every time!

Consider a typical scenario that happens to me on virtually every shot: you take a few practice swings, and the last one is perfect. Your hips turn properly, your head stays down, you roll your wrist perfectly, you just skim the top of the grass, and your follow through is elegantly balanced. If you only used that last practice swing, it would've been a perfect shot. Then, you step up to the ball and try to duplicate that one perfect practice swing. In a matter of microseconds, before you even strike the ball, you know something is very wrong. Your backswing didn't go back far enough, or you lifted your head, or you bent your left elbow, or you thought about maybe hitting it too hard or too soft, or maybe the small body of water nearby suddenly crept into your swing thoughts. Way too many swing thoughts. So, after the massive brain pollution has completely skewed your swing, your ball goes somewhere. If you're fortunate, the ball goes where you had originally intended for it to go. Sometimes it does, but the majority of the time for us high handicappers the ball goes elsewhere. Then, if you're like me, you begin what could be described as a horrible, mostly embarrassing melodramatic temper tantrum, which typically involves screaming, cursing, wailing, and gnashing of teeth, and even some Olympic-level club tossing.

We all have varying degrees of temperament on the golf course. Some people are actually very calm and tolerant of any bad shot – like my friend Greg. I'm not one of them. Even the best professional golfers have been seen throwing clubs or cursing a blue streak after a poor shot. Funny irony, as I'm writing this, I see the number one golfer in the world just barely miss a putt for par in the U.S. Open. The putt was not at all considered a gimme. It was, in fact, about a 25-footer with a right-to-left break on a rock-hard, very fast green. He missed the putt by inches. This usually very calm and poised man flipped his putter in the air in frustration, ultimately landing on the green. When we mere mortals witness a professional golfer hitting a bad shot or throwing a bit of a temper tantrum, we sometimes feel a sense of kindred spirit with them. I'm quite certain that when he settles down a bit, he'll regret his brief lapse in patience and good sportsmanship. He might even be a bit embarrassed. I know the feeling well. This game will humble even the best golfers in the world. It can, quite literally bring you to your knees.

Mad About Me

Have you ever wondered why we get so angry after a bad shot? Can you name any other sport that elicits such raw emotions in us? Baseball can be frustrating, but I would argue, not anything like golf. One of the worst feelings in baseball is to strike out. I remember all sorts of anger whenever I struck out in Little League, but nothing like the anger and frustration after hitting a bad golf shot. I remember missing many free throws in basketball, dropping passes in football, missing shots on goal in soccer. I can't think of any sport that even comes close to comparing it to the frustration of a bad golf shot.

So, the other day I was golfing with Carolyn. Carolyn is almost the polar opposite of me when it comes to intensity in sporting events. She'll play any sport for fun; win, lose, draw, it doesn't matter. She does get a little dangerous at card games, and she might rip your face off (not literally) in a game of Farkle, or Liars Dice but these games are outliers for her. She is usually very calm.

Golf is a totally different animal. Suddenly, she becomes one of us. We were out playing a round of golf on a very beautiful day. Wispy white clouds dotting the blue sky, low humidity, perfect temperature. We tee off, so far so good, right? We get to the second shot and go through the predictable pre-shot routine. Sure enough, two good practice strokes she then steps up to hit the real shot. She tops it, and the ball bounces a bit. Then, it comes to a stop about 10 yards from where she hit it. After saying some audibly unkind words to the ball, she returns to the cart. I said, "Carolyn, let me ask you a question, you are normally a low intensity person, nothing really gets you riled. Why do you get so angry after hitting a bad shot?"

Her answer was quick and simple. "I just want to be good at this." Hmmm, interesting.

We all want to be good and do good, don't we? After our preparation and formation, we come to this game with high expectations or, at the very least, with optimism. We are full of excitement and anticipation. As in life, we know the importance of doing good and being good. God tells us, "You shall therefore be holy, for I am holy." [111] and Jesus adds, "You, therefore, must be

---

[111] Lev 11:45.

perfect, as your heavenly Father is perfect." [112] This can seem like quite a daunting task. How in the world can we be perfect in life? How in the world can we be perfect in golf? Admittedly, perfection in golf is a little less daunting than perfection in the eyes of God, but it is challenging to say the least. For one hole, perfection is generally defined as a hole-in-one. For 18 holes, perfection might be defined as a birdie or better on each hole. Not easy, right? Hebrews gives us a hint. "Look to Jesus the pioneer and perfecter of our faith, who for the joy that was set before him endured the cross, despising the shame, and is seated at the right hand of the throne of God."[113]

It may be more about *how* we get to perfect, that is, what are we doing and thinking on the journey? We may need to revisit humility once again. "In his *Spiritual Exercises*, St Ignatius describes three kinds of humility:

- To humble myself to total obedience to God
- To be ready for honor or dishonor, poverty or wealth, or anything else for God
- To desire poverty, dishonor, and even be a fool for God, since Christ was."[114]

This is some of the best advice for golfers – especially me. I need to be ready to handle the great shots **and** the bad shots, the honor or dishonor, poverty or wealth, or anything else for God. I need to swallow my pride and be the fool when I remove a foot-long chunk of turf while chipping.

The Water Hazard is a Mortal Sin

Sin, as described in the Catechism, goes like this: "An offense against God as well as a fault against reason, truth, and right conscience. Sin is a deliberate thought, word, deed, or omission contrary to the eternal law of God. In judging the gravity of sin, it is customary to distinguish between mortal and venial sin.:[115] Mortal sin is described as: "A grave infraction of the law of God that destroys the divine life in the soul."[116] Three conditions must be met

---

[112] Mt 5:48.

[113] Heb 12:2.

[114] Tim Muldoon, *Three Kinds of Humility,* (Ignatianspirituality.com).

[115] CCC Glossary, 766.

[116] CCC Glossary, 757.

for a sin to be a mortal sin: "Mortal sin is sin whose object is **grave matter** and which is also committed with **full knowledge** and **deliberate consent**."[117]

So, we address the ball and determine (full knowledge) that we have no earthly chance of clearing the water hazard. We hit it anyway (deliberate consent), and our ball flies into the water hazard (grave matter). By definition, a mortal sin was committed. Interesting, huh? Can we connect this little example to our life, remembering that the golf ball represents our eternal soul? Sin represents a turning away from God; if the golf ball is our soul, it has just been terminally separated from our target – the hole.

Author's note: Hitting a golf ball into a water hazard is not really a mortal sin, although sometimes it might seem like it.

Sounds not only dire, but terminal, right? In golf when we lose the ball it's game over. In life, when we lose our soul, the game is over. Praise the Lord that we have a good and merciful God. And the Rules of Golf.

In golf, we have as many second chances as we have golf balls in our bag. But we also have the Rules of Golf. To illustrate how the rules of golf provide relief, shall we say, forgiveness, and help us stay on our journey toward the hole, let's use the ball hit into the water hazard as an example.

"Rule 17.1d Relief for ball in penalty area. If a player's ball is in a penalty area, including when it is known or virtually certain to be in a penalty area even though not found, the player has these relief options, each for one penalty stroke:
1. Stroke and distance relief. The player may play the original ball or another ball from where the previous stroke was made.
2. Back on the line relief. The player may drop the original ball or another ball outside the penalty area, keeping the estimated point where the original ball last crossed the edge of the penalty area between the hole and the spot where the ball is dropped..."[118]

In layman's terms, this means you can continue on your journey by dropping another ball (or, if you can, retrieve the one in the water)

---

[117] CCC ¶ 1857.
[118] USGA.org.

and keep playing. This is a freely gifted grace, is it not? Well, technically, it's not totally free. We probably lost the original ball, and it did cost us a penalty stroke, more on this "cost" later.

This seems very similar to what happens in the Confessional. When we fall into grave sin on our journey of life, we need to seek relief. Mortal sin severely injures our relationship with God; the sacrament of Reconciliation heals that injury.

When our first parents, Adam and Eve, ate of the "tree of the knowledge of good and evil,"[119] our lives changed even before we were born. The Catechism says, "All men are implicated in Adam's sin, as St. Paul affirms: 'By one man's disobedience many [that is, all men] were made sinners': sin came into the world through one man and death through sin, and so death spread to all men because all men sinned."[120] But, St Paul continues with, "Then as one man's trespass led to condemnation for all men, so one man's (Christ) act of righteousness leads to acquittal and life for all men."[121] Ahh, relief from the hazard(s).

"Those who approach the sacrament of Penance (Reconciliation) obtain pardon from God's mercy for the offense committed against him, and are, at the same time reconciled with the Church which they have wounded by their sins and which by charity, by example and by prayer labors for their conversions."[122] This is awesome; we are reconciled with the Church, too? Yes. Our faith and sin are personal but not private. Our sins also wound the people around us.

If we apply the sacrament of Reconciliation to our golf ball in the water, this is our free drop. We get a brand new ball. In life, we begin anew, and we are able to continue our journey to Heaven. We experience the free gift of grace. But remember, as with the Rules of Golf, our free gift is not entirely free. There is a "cost." Our sins are forgiven, and our ***eternal*** punishment has been removed, but often, there are ***temporal*** punishments to deal with. Temporal punishments might best be described as disciplinary lessons. As James Akin states, "Why does God leave or implement some

---

[119] Gn 2:17.
[120] CCC ¶ 402. Cf Rom 5:12,19.
[121] Rom 5:18.
[122] CCC ¶ 1422.

temporal penalties in place when he removes the eternal penalties for our sins? Part of this is a mystery since Christ's sufferings are surely sufficient to cover even the temporal penalties of our sins. However, one reason is to teach us our lesson."[123] There is precedence for this in Scripture as well. Moses and David, among many others, were both punished temporally when God called out their disobedience. Moses was not allowed to enter the Promised Land, and David lost a son. James Akin continues with this from Hebrews: "'My son, do not regard lightly the discipline of the Lord, nor lose courage when you are punished by Him. For the Lord disciplines him whom he loves and chastises every son whom he receives.' It is for discipline that you have to endure. God is treating you as sons; for what son is there whom his father does not discipline?'"[124]

Many times, when we receive our "penance" from the priest in confession, it is generally in the form of doing good works or prayers. These subtle disciplines from our Father teach lessons. The lost golf ball and the one-stroke penalty are our temporal punishments in the game of golf.

---

[123] James Akin, *Catechism and Apologetics*, (EWTM.co.uk, May, 13, 2022).
[124] Heb 12:5-7.

Did You Know?

There are a couple of interesting aspects to Reconciliation. The first is about temporal punishment and the other is about the unforgiveable sin. When the priest gives a penance of, say, three Hail Mary's or maybe an Our Father, this penance is not intended to be some rigorous discipline or penalty. Or worse, it is not intended to be a meaningless exercise. It is meant to change our hearts. The temporal aspect of our sin is sometimes described as a stain. The sacrament of Reconciliation removes the sin, but the stain remains.

Another way to envision this is to imagine hammering nails into a piece of wood. Reconciliation removes the nails, but the holes in the wood are still there. The stain, or the holes in the wood, is our attachment to sin.

Did you know that performing penance, changing our hearts, assists in the removal of the temporal stain of sin? Fasting, prayers, almsgiving, and Eucharistic Adoration are all forms of penance that enhance our conversion of heart toward God.

The unforgivable sin is the sin we don't confess. The Catechism says, "Confession to a priest is an essential part of the sacrament of Penance, 'for if the sick person is too ashamed to show his wound to the doctor, the medicine cannot heal what it does not know.'"[125]

Jesus goes further: "Truly, I say to you, all sins will be forgiven the sons of men, and whatever blasphemies they utter; but whoever blasphemes against the Holy Spirit never has forgiveness, but is guilty of an eternal sin."[126] Did you know that God knows all our sins? He wants us to acknowledge them—to ourselves. "In Confession, you're not telling Him what He doesn't know, you're giving Him access to what He doesn't have… your heart". – Fr. Mike Schmitz.

---

[125] CCC ¶ 1456, Cf St. Jerome, *In Eccl.* 10.
[126] Mk 3:28-30.

EIGHT
On the Green

(The Anointing of the Sick)

The Sacraments of Reconciliation and Anointing of the Sick go hand in hand. They are both sacraments of healing. Spiritual healing, for sure, and sometimes physical healing. As we methodically progress through our own "Fairway to Heaven" and suffer through our "Water Hazards," we eventually and finally reach the green. There are a couple of sacramental thoughts that come to mind once we land the ball on the green – we are very close to the end of our journey toward the "Target", but there is still much that can happen before the ball goes into the hole.

The End is coming

One of the most enduring mysteries of life is the end times. When is it going to happen? When is Jesus coming back? Jesus himself said, "But of that day and hour no one knows, not even the angels of heaven, nor the Son, but the Father only."[127] For nearly all of us, the second coming of Jesus will take place long after our own life has ended. When our golf ball has reached the green, we can almost see the end. We are so close that we can virtually see the ball go into the hole with our very next putt. This may be as close as we get to predicting the end, at least in golf.

In life, there are some circumstances where we can get reasonably close, right? Fr. Bob, in a homily on Mt 24:36, said we could predict our end if, for example, we are a death-row prisoner. This is a case where we could literally tag the time of death within seconds. For most of us though, being a death-row prisoner is not happening. For most of us, even if we've made it to the "putting

---

[127] Mt 24:36.

surface" of life, we still can't predict our end with a high degree of confidence.

The Anointing of the Green

When our ball is finally on the green, we experience several very positive effects. We feel strong and confident, we're at peace, and we are encouraged that we overcame the difficulties to get there. We have a sense of unity with the game itself – we've arrived – we're on the "dance floor". We celebrate our "arrival" because it benefits not only our personal journey but that of our golf buddy. And finally, as we line up that last and final putt, we are confident in all that we've done to get here.

The effects of the Anointing of the Sick mirror, to a large degree, the effects of our reaching the green. According to the Catechism:

- The first grace of this sacrament is one of strengthening, peace and courage to overcome the difficulties.[128]
- By the grace of this sacrament the sick person receives the strength and the gift of uniting himself more closely to Christ's Passion.[129]
- The sick who receive this sacrament, "by freely uniting themselves to the passion and death of Christ, contribute to the good of the People of God.[130]
- This last anointing fortifies the end of our earthly life like a solid rampart for the final struggles before entering the Father's house.[131]

The Dreaded 3-Putt

Beyond the more obvious aspects of the Anointing of the Sick, imminent death, another aspect to consider is the illness of an individual. This sacrament is often called the sacrament of the sick. The Catechism describes it like this. "The Church believes and confesses that among the seven sacraments there is one especially intended to strengthen those who are being tried by illness, the

---

[128] CCC ¶ 1520.
[129] CCC ¶ 1521.
[130] CCC ¶ 1522.
[131] CCC ¶ 1523.

Anointing of the Sick:

'This sacred anointing of the sick was instituted by Christ our Lord as a true and proper sacrament of the New Testament. It is alluded to indeed by Mark but is recommended to the faithful and promulgated by James the apostle and brother of the Lord.'"[132]

As we all know, you haven't finished your round until the ball is in the hole. In our exercise of analogy between the game of golf and life, having finally reached the green can be analogous to our "preparation for the final journey"[133] in life. Hence, a missed putt, regardless of how many putts it takes to finally sink it, can be reasonably described as an illness of sorts – some would argue the "yips" are both a physical and mental illness.

"Heal the sick!"[134] "The Church has received this charge from the Lord and strives to carry it out by taking care of the sick as well as by accompanying them with her prayer of intercession. She believes in the life-giving presence of Christ, the physician of souls and bodies."[135]

"The apostolic Church has its own rite for the sick attested to by St. James: 'Is any among you sick? Let him call for the elders of the Church and let them pray over him, anointing him with oil in the name of the Lord; and the prayer of faith will save the sick man, and the Lord will raise him up; and if he has committed sins, he will be forgiven. Tradition has recognized in this rite one of the seven sacraments."[136]

Keeping with the analogy and remembering that the golf ball equates to our soul when we are on the green looking over the crucial putt that can ensure that we reach our target, we might experience symptoms of weakness. Perhaps knee-knocking nervousness, sweaty palms, a strong drain of confidence – the yips! It is times like these that we would do well to remember what the Catechism says about the sacrament: "The Anointing of the Sick is not a sacrament for those only who are at the point of death. Hence, as soon as anyone of the faithful begins to be in danger of death from sickness

---

[132] CCC ¶ 1511.
[133] CCC ¶ 1523.
[134] Mt 10:8.
[135] CCC ¶ 1509.
[136] CCC ¶ 1510.

or old age, the fitting time for him to receive this sacrament has certainly already arrived."[137]

The special grace of this sacrament has the effects of "uniting us with the passion of Christ... strengthening the peace and courage to endure the sufferings of illness or old age in a Christian manner... forgiveness of sins... restoration of health, if it is conducive to his/her salvation... preparing for the passing over to eternal life."[138]

Celebrating Unfulfilled Dreams

When we've successfully made it to the green, it is also a good time to reflect on what just happened. How did we get here? What happened along the way? What is still ahead in the very near future?

On a recent vacation, my eldest son Joseph gave me a couple of small books to read at my leisure. One of the books, *Wrestling With God – Finding Hope And Meaning In Our Daily Struggle To Be Human*, by Ronald Rolheiser,[139] was particularly interesting because the author struck a nerve in me. It helped me view my patience and anger issues when hitting poor shots in a different light.

Rolheiser posits a metaphorical Old Testament story about the Gileadite named Jephthah in the book of Judges.[140] Jephthah is asked to lead Israel in war against the Ammonites in the story. At some point in the battle, things aren't going well. Jephthah prays to God and vows that if he should be victorious, he promises God that the first person who enters his house to greet him will be offered to God as a burnt offering. Well, as God would have it, Jephthah was victorious. But, the first person to enter his house was his virgin daughter and only child. Chalk this one up to be careful what you ask for! Jephthah's daughter, to her credit, insists that her dad fulfill his promise to God. She only asks that she first be allowed to join her other virgin friends in a two-month wandering in the mountains to "bewail my virginity."[141] She did her thing and came back resolved to live out the rest of her life—a very short rest of her life—as a virgin.

---

[137] CCC ¶ 1514.
[138] CCC ¶ 1532.
[139] Ronald Rolheiser, *Wrestling with God*, (Image Publishing, 2018).
[140] Judges 11:1-40.
[141] Judges 11:37.

Rolheiser's point, at least as directed toward me, is that I should "bewail" or mourn my bad shots and then move on. I should practice my humility, ready to honor or dishonor or be a fool for God. As former professional NFL quarterback Philip Rivers often says, *"Nunc Coepi,"* Now I Begin.

Bad shots will happen; 3-putts will happen. Sometimes we are healed "and they cast out many demons, and anointed with oil many that were sick and healed them."[142] Sometimes we are not healed, "my grace is sufficient for you, for my power is made perfect in weakness."[143] So goes the mystery of our journey. The Gospel of John also makes this point in the Good Shepherd discourse: "I came that they may have life and have it abundantly."[144] Fr. Bob asks two questions: "What is Jesus' version of abundant life? What is our version of abundant life?" We mere humans might say that abundant life is health, wealth, security, and family happiness. But Jesus, as Fr. Bob reminds us, didn't preach on happiness. He preached the beatitudes. "I didn't say it would be easy, but I promise it will be worth it."

---

142 Mk 6:13.
143 2Cor 12:9.
144 Jn 10:10.

Did You Know?

The Anointing of the Sick was formerly called Extreme Unction, meaning Final Anointing. The Catechism explains it this way: "Over the centuries the Anointing of the Sick was conferred more and more exclusively on those at the point of death. Because of this, it received the name 'Extreme Unction'. Notwithstanding this evolution, the liturgy has never failed to beg the Lord that the sick person may recover his health if it would be conducive to his salvation."[145]

This is surely another reason why we can't accurately predict our end. If it be God's will, we shall be around a little longer.

---

[145] CCC ¶ 1512.

NINE
It's in the Hole

(The Target)

The game of golf, from tee to green, is a microcosm of life on the journey to salvation. The sacraments follow us on this journey, even on the golf course. Maybe especially on the golf course. Bishop Barren said, "The Sacraments are the preparation for Heaven."[146] The sacraments prepare us for the moment we will see God face-to-face. The graces we receive through the sacraments, as we mature through life, are affirmed by God.

In another homily by Fr. Bob, he reminded us that God, on three occasions, spoke to us in Scripture affirming His grace. At the time of Jesus' baptism, "This is my beloved Son, with whom I am well pleased."[147] At the Transfiguration, "This is my beloved Son, with whom I am well pleased; listen to Him."[148] And again, when Jesus entered Jerusalem, "I have glorified it, and I will glorify it again."[149] We experience this affirmation of grace in all of the sacraments, particularly in the Eucharist and Reconciliation where we see Him face-to-face, through the priests, and experience His love much more directly.

Earlier, we talked about perfection and how daunting a task that is. Remember "You, therefore, must be perfect, as your heavenly Father is perfect"?[150] Recall that Jesus' last words were, "It is finished."[151] Various translations have their meaning as "it is complete, it is perfected." Jesus affirmed that all He was sent to

---

[146] Father Mike Schmitz, Podcast, (Ascension Presents, 2024).
[147] Mt 3:17.
[148] Mt 17:5.
[149] Jn 12:28.
[150] Mt 5:48.
[151] Jn 19:30.

accomplish was achieved. That is what I say as my ball drops into the hole. It is finished!

Faith is Simple, But Not Easy

There is a very large, and by all accounts, a very successful Catholic parish in Timonium, Maryland, Church of the Nativity. They coined the phrase, "Churching is Simple, But Not Easy." And, boy are they correct! This phrase is directed toward volunteerism in parishes and the inner workings of ministry organization, but I think the paraphrase is also valid. Faith is Simple, But Not Easy. When you sink a long birdie putt or hit that rare hole-in-one, golf seems like an easy sport, right? But, most of the time, when you finally put the ball in the hole, you've just completed an arduous journey. If you took time to reflect on the journey, you would quickly realize it wasn't all that easy. It takes a fitness that is both physical and mental. It takes a great faith in your instructions and your execution of those instructions.

It takes great faith to succeed. Remembering Fr. Richard Simon's, "Faith equals Trust." Pierre Teilhard de Chardin, a Jesuit priest, composed a prayer that sums up beautifully the process of trust:

Patient Trust[152]

Above all, trust in the slow work of God. We are quite naturally impatient in everything to reach the end without delay.

We should like to skip the intermediate stages. We are impatient of being on the way to something unknown, something new.

And yet it is the law of all progress that it is made by passing through some stages of instability—and that it may take a very long time.

And so I think it is with you; your ideas mature gradually—let them grow, let them shape themselves, without undue haste.

---

[152] Pierre Teilhard de Chardin, *Patient Trust*, Excerpts from Hearts on Fire. Ignationspirituality.com.

Don't try to force them on as though you could be today what time (that is to say, grace and circumstances acting on your own good will) will make of you tomorrow.

Only God could say what this new spirit gradually forming within you will be.

Give Our Lord the benefit of believing that his hand is leading you, and accept the anxiety of feeling yourself in suspense and incomplete.

Every time I read this prayer, I'm reminded how pertinent it is to my golf game—the slow work of God, indeed!

Another really good example of great faith is Fr. Mike Schmitz's homily on the Canaanite woman in Matthew 15:21-28.[153] His lesson is, "Only faith that is tested can become great."[154] This, too, is a lesson for life and golf. Fr. Mike lists four tests that define great faith, and all four tests are illustrated in this Gospel. These are tests that all Christians face repeatedly in their journey.

To set the scene, you have this Canaanite woman with a sick daughter; the daughter is possessed by a demon. She comes to Jesus with a good thing. She has human love. She is armed with the love a mother has for her child. But human love cannot save a soul, so Jesus wants her to have something better, faith in Him.

The tests of her faith begin with the prayer, "Have mercy on me, O Lord, Son of David; my daughter is severely possessed by a demon."[155] What was Jesus' response? Silence.

The first test: Silence. It seems as though Jesus doesn't hear our prayer.

She persists, this time with the disciples. Then what happens? The disciples came begging Jesus, "Send her away, for she is crying after us."[156] So, her first encounter with Christians resulted in them begging Jesus to send her away.

The second test: Rejection. We ask fellow Christians for help and they don't have time for us.

---

[153] Mt 15:21-28.

[154] Fr. Mike Schmitz, *Father Mike's Sunday Homily*, (Ascension Presents, YouTube, Aug. 18, 2020).

[155] Mt 15:22.

[156] Mt 15:23.

Then Jesus finally answers the woman and says, "I was sent only to the lost sheep of the house of Israel."[157]

The third test. This sounds like a No. Is Jesus really saying "NO" to our prayer?

Then, after the woman prayed more, Jesus said, "It is not fair to take the children's bread and throw it to the dogs."[158] Did Jesus just call her a dog?

The fourth test. Does Jesus even care? I am confused by what God is telling me.

The real questions are: Do I have great faith? Is it a faith different from others that don't have "great" faith? Does my faith make any difference to how I act? Has the faith I profess caused me to live differently?

This woman, through all the "negative" vibes and discouragement, trusted that Jesus was going to ultimately answer her prayer. She says, "Yes, Lord, yet even the dogs eat the crumbs that fall from their masters' table."[159] "Then Jesus answered her, 'O woman, great is your faith! Let it be done for you as you desire.' And her daughter was healed instantly."[160] Can you imagine how awesome her "great" faith was, especially when we consider that Peter was rebuked for having, "O you of little faith."?[161]

This story is an example of the little pop quizzes that all Christians face many times while on the journey. I would argue that these same types of testing happen during every round of golf.

Faith, Hope, and a Gimme

"Virtue is an habitual and firm disposition to do good."[162] Carolyn demonstrated virtue when she proclaimed, "I just want to be good at this." There are human virtues and there are theological virtues. "The human virtues are rooted in the theological virtues, which adapt man's faculties for participation in the divine nature: for the theological virtues relate directly to God. They dispose

---

[157] Mt 15:24.
[158] Mt 15:26.
[159] Mt 15:27.
[160] Mt 15:28.
[161] Mt 14:31.
[162] CCC ¶ 1803.

Christians to live in a relationship with the Holy Trinity. They have the One and Triune God for their origin, motive, and object."[163]

"There are three theological virtues: faith, hope, and charity (love)."[164] We've already discussed faith in some detail, we believe in God and all that He has revealed to us. Hope is the virtue, "by which we desire the kingdom of heaven and eternal life as our happiness, placing our trust in Christ's promises and relying not on our own strength, but on the help of the grace of the Holy Spirit."[165]

We can readily see the connection between these two virtues and the game of golf, right? Faith in instruction and faith in practice lead to our hope of success of achieving the target.

Love is the virtue, "by which we love God above all things for his own sake, and our neighbor as ourselves for the love of God."[166] We demonstrate love by the way we play and appreciate the game of golf. Encouragement for our partners and from our partners. Maintaining and following the Rules of Golf and appreciating God's gift of pristine golf courses, and the natural beauty of the scenery.

A gimme is a slangy shortening of "give me". It is a nice gesture from a golf partner that allows a stroke to be counted, without actually making the stroke. For example, if your partner has a short putt, many times you will just "give" them that putt so they don't actually have to hit it. While not technically a virtue, a gimme could be considered a member of the love family of virtues, yes?

In life and golf, the three virtues have the same life cycle. From tee to green, we exercise and demonstrate our faith, hope, and love, right up to the moment the ball goes into the hole. Same in our daily lives. When the ball goes into the hole, or when we arrive at our particular day of judgment, faith and hope cease to exist for us. The only virtue that continues is love. Love is in our souls because we were conceived in God's love and the love of our parents.

St. John of the Cross was quoted as saying, "So many of the things we do to rank ourselves as being successes or failures will not matter at all…. In the twilight of our lives God will not judge us on

---

[163]CCC ¶ 1812.
[164] CCC ¶ 1813.
[165] CCC ¶ 1817.
[166] CCC ¶ 1822.

our earthly possessions and our human success, but rather on how much we have loved."[167]

When we have reached our target and achieved our goal, our faith and hope are done, and we no longer need them. The one thing left, and the only thing we take with us, is love—love of the game, love of life, and love of God—it is complete, it is perfected, and it is finished!

---

[167] St. John of the Cross, www.azquotes.com .

Did You Know?

If you believe in miracles, you'll love this one. The feast of Our Lady of Guadalupe is celebrated every year on December 12th. There were many miracles associated with the Marian apparitions at Tepeyac Hill near Mexico City, Mexico, in December 1531, not the least of which were the apparitions themselves. The Castilian roses, the image of our Blessed Mother on the tilma of Juan Diego, and the cure of Juan Diego's uncle are among the most notable miracles reported during that moment in time.

But did you know the tilma has been subjected to nearly as many examinations by painters, restoration specialists, and forensic scientists as the shroud of Turin? One of the most unusual claims involved the examination of Mary's eyes. The scientists who have studied the eyes claim they have found images in the eyes that "correspond to the people believed to have been present when Juan Diego unfolded his tilma before Bishop Zumarraga."[168] The eyes depict an image of the group of people who would be looking at the tilma as Juan Diego was unfolding it. "More recently, an engineer named Dr. Jose Aste Tonsmann, who began his studies on Our Lady of Guadalupe's eyes in 1979, said there are many more figures reflected in her gaze."[169]

Can you imagine being one of those people in the room? Can you imagine being in the same room with our Blessed Mother?

What if it was Jesus? What would Jesus see? When we talk about the end times – when we finally see the face of God – I'm mindful of this miracle at Guadalupe. It also brings to mind what Jesus said about the final judgment:

"When the Son of man comes in his glory, and all the angels with him, then he will sit on his glorious throne. Before him will be gathered all the nations, and he will separate them one from another as a shepherd separates the sheep from the goats, and he will place the sheep at his right hand but the goats at the left. Then the King will say to those at his right hand, 'Come, O blessed of my Father, inherit the kingdom prepared for you from the foundation of the

---

[168] Our Lady of Guadalupe, Wekipedia.org.

[169] Get Fed, The Catholic Company, <u>What image is Hidden in the Eyes of Our Lady of Guadalupe?</u>. Dec 12, 2024.

world; for I was hungry and you gave me food, I was thirsty and you gave me drink, I was a stranger and your welcomed me, I was naked and you clothed me, I was sick and you visited me, I was in prison and you came to me.' Then the righteous will answer him, 'Lord, when did we see you hungry and feed you, or thirsty and give you drink? And when did we see you a stranger and welcome you, or naked and clothe you? And when did we see you sick or in prison and visit you?' And the King will answer them, 'Truly, I say to you, as you did it to one of the least of these my brethren, you did it to me.'"[170]

So, as we continue the journey toward our target, we don't have to wait to see the face of God, we can do it today and every day. As St. Mother Teresa of Calcutta says, "We are called to be contemplatives – devoted to prayer – by seeking the face of God in everything, everyone, everywhere, all the time."[171]

---

[170] Mt 25:31-40.
[171] Mother Teresa, www.azquotes.com.

TEN
The Rose Garden

(The Holy Rosary)

If you've made it this far, you are most likely a golfer; you've played several rounds, or you have at least heard of the game. Hopefully, you will agree my case has been made. Golf is truly universal – big "C" Catholic – and the Sacraments are thoroughly embedded into every aspect of the game.

Let's Pray A Round

So, if the sacraments help us participate in God's free gift of grace, what do you think prayer does? Well, for one thing, we are commanded to pray, right? St. Paul tells us, "Rejoice always, pray constantly, give thanks in all circumstances; for this is the will of God in Christ Jesus for you."[172] I'm sure you have heard it said several times; to pray is to converse with God. During a round of golf, many conversations with God occur. Some of these conversations are full of hope, praise and thanksgiving, and some – not so much.

To bring our golf-imitates-life analogy full circle, a round of golf can also be compared to the Holy Rosary. Yep. The rosary is *round*, and it gets its name, in part, from "the Latin word *rosarium* which is used to describe a rose garden."[173] Which, of course, recalls the Garden of Eden, our first golf course.

To be clear, the rosary is not a sacrament, but it is considered a *sacramental*. Wait, what's a sacramental? The Catechism defines sacramentals as follows:

"Holy Mother Church has, moreover, instituted sacramentals. These are sacred signs which bear a resemblance to the sacraments.

---

[172] 1Th 5:16-18.
[173] Donald H. Calloway, MIC, *Champions of the Rosary*, (Marian Press,2016), 39.

They signify effects, particularly of a spiritual nature, which are obtained through the intersession of the Church. By them men are disposed to receive the chief effect of the sacraments, and various occasions in life are rendered holy."[174]

Blessings, the intercessions of the Church, are the "secret sauce" of a sacramental. The blessing by a bishop or priest is what changes a string of beads into a rosary. Sacramentals are, what I like to call, the genius of Catholicism, that is to say, the genius of God. Through the Church's teaching authority, the Magisterium, granted by Jesus himself,[175] we are the beneficiaries of these wonderful "helps" that "prepare us to receive grace and dispose us to cooperate with it."[176]

The origins of the present-day rosary can be traced to the ministry of St. Dominic in the 13th century. Before the rosary got its name, the earliest form of this prayer "was called the Psalter of Mary, because as the Davidic Psalter is composed of 150 Psalms, so also in the rosary we find 150 Hail Marys."[177] Even before the Hail Mary, the laity substituted the Psalms for the Lord's Prayer, referred to as the Our Father (Paternoster). Eventually, 150 beads were strung together for the purpose of keeping track of the number of Our Fathers prayed. These were called Paternoster beads. This provided an accessible method for individuals without financial resources or means to emulate the daily prayers of monks and clergy. Centuries before St. Dominic, monks were required to pray the 150 Psalms daily, but most people could not afford a printed version of the Psalms, and literacy was low, even among the clergy, so they couldn't read them anyway.

In his book, *Champions of the Rosary*, describing the origins of the rosary as a spiritual weapon, Fr. Donald H. Calloway, MIC, says: "After all of the pieces had been brought together in the 12th century—the Hail Mary, the Our Father, prayer beads, and the Marian Psalter—the sword was ready to be assembled and entrusted to a man who would be forever known as its founder."[178] St. Dominic was that man. He took these components, and added his

---

[174] CCC ¶ 1667.
[175] Mt 28:18-20. Lk 10:16. Mt 18:18.
[176] CCC ¶ 1670.
[177] Donald H. Calloway, MIC, *Champions of the Rosary*, (Marian Press, 2016), 40.
[178] Ibid., 33.

"meditative method of preaching on the sacred mysteries of the life of Christ."[179] Fr. Calloway injects some additional context:

"God always intended his weapon to be a Marian sword since he knew the woman and her children would be under attack. It was fitting, then, that the first element to be poured into the mold was the sweet *Ave: "Hail, full of grace, the Lord is with you."* This divinely inspired announcement, uttered first by the Archangel Gabriel, is known as the Angelic Salutation."[180] Fr. Calloway continues:

"The Catholic Church is the workshop that the Divine Craftsman used to assemble the sword. As God Almighty, he could have constructed the sword in one act. However, since the construction of the sword was to occur in time, he allowed for the gathering of the elements in his workshop to take centuries. For example, it was not until the sixth century that the Catholic Church combined the *Angelic Salutation* with the *Evangelical Salutation*. The Evangelical Salutation is the inspired greeting of St. Elizabeth to Mary: *"Blessed are you among women, and blessed is the fruit of your womb!"*[181]

There is a sad irony regarding the rosary, and it involves the prayer itself. The rosary has always been a very Catholic prayer and devotion. Considering its origin – established well before the Reformation. It is hard to argue that point; virtually all of Christianity was considered Catholic prior to the 1500s. Beginning with the Reformation and the 500+ years following, many of our brothers and sisters in Christ left the Catholic Church. As a result, customs and practices associated with Catholicism were dismissed as heretical, or worse. The doctrine of *sola scriptura,* one of the basic tenets of the Reformation, had a drastically negative effect on the practice of structured prayer, the rosary, for example. It's sad because the foundational prayers of the rosary, the Lord's Prayer and the Hail Mary, are deeply rooted in Scripture.

---

[179] Ibid., 38.
[180] Ibid., 28-29.
[181] Ibid.

The Hail Mary

"Hail [Mary] full of grace, the Lord is with you."[182] *"Blessed are you among women, and blessed is the fruit of your womb, [Jesus]."*[183]

The Lord's Prayer

"Our Father who are in heaven, hallowed be thy name. Thy kingdom come, thy will be done on earth as it is in heaven. Give us this day our daily bread; and forgive us our trespasses as we forgive those who trespass against us; and lead us not into temptation, but deliver us from evil."[184]

The Sacred Mysteries, Joyful, Sorrowful, Luminous and Glorious, are meditations on the very life of Jesus. These mysteries are the Gospels. So, while the Lord's Prayer and the Hail Mary are the foundational prayers recited, it is in the meditation on the life of Jesus that makes this prayer so fruitful.

A fun fact about the second half of the Hail Mary was articulated by Bishop Sheen.

"This [the second half of the Hail Mary] was not introduced until the latter part of the Middle Ages. Since it seizes upon the two decisive moments of life: "now" and "at the hour of our death," it suggests the spontaneous outcry of people in a great calamity. The Black Death, which ravaged all of Europe and wiped out one-third of its population, prompted the faithful to cry out to the Mother of Our Lord to protect them at a time when the present moment and death were almost one."[185]

Holy Mary, Mother of God, pray for us sinners, now and at the hour of our death, Amen.

Why do we ask Mary to pray for us? Why do we ask *anyone* to pray for us? Scripture tells us to "bear one another's burdens, and so fulfill the law of Christ."[186] The model for this intercessory prayer comes from two very famous Queen Mothers. Bathsheba, on behalf

---

[182] Lk 1:28.
[183] Lk 1:42.
[184] Mt 6:9-13.
[185] Donald H. Calloway, MIC, *Champions of the Rosary*, (Marian Press,2016), 53
[186] Gal 6:2.

of Adonijah, petitioned her son King Solomon[187]; and Mary, on behalf of the wedding party at Cana, petitioned her son Jesus – King of the Universe.[188]

A Walk in the Garden

As stated earlier, the rosary has long been associated with roses, "a grouping of roses in a wreath or a bouquet."[189] In his podcast, The Rosary in a Year, Fr. Mark-Mary Ames, merges this historical "rose garden" with Old Testament Scripture to form an image of today's rosary. In the Song of Solomon, "I am a rose of Sharon, a lily of the valleys."[190] In this verse, we hear a typological image of Mary as the rose. Fr. Mark-Mary completes the picture, comparing our praying the rosary to "spending time walking in the garden of Jesus with Mary."[191] He captures the image of a safe, clean, beautiful space full of fresh flowers and lush green grass.

As we reflect on the rosary we can find a spiritual parallel between our "sacramental" journey on the golf course and the journey of Jesus during his earthly ministry. Our "sacramental" journey began at *Baptism* when we joined the "club". We grew in wisdom and knowledge of the game through the *Holy Orders* and *Confirmation* process of instruction, formation, and proper equipment. We were nourished and sustained by the *Eucharist,* and perhaps an adult beverage. We found friendship, counsel, fellowship, and a lifetime partner as we paired up in *Matrimony*. We learned right from wrong and paid the "cost" of our mistakes through *Reconciliation*. Finally, we were healed by the *Anointing of the Sick* as we reached the "green" of life. We were lifted up as we "hit" the target on the last hole.

The rosary *is* the journey of Jesus. These are the Mysteries:[192]

---

[187] 1 Kgs 2:18-20.

[188] Jn 2:5.

[189] Donald H. Calloway, MIC, *Champions of the Rosary*, (Marian Press,2016), 27-33.

[190] Song of Solomon 2:1.

[191] Fr. Mark-Mary, *The Rosary in a Year podcast*, (Ascension Press), 2025.

[192] Donald H. Calloway, MIC, *Champions of the Rosary*, (Marian Press,2016), Excerpts 339-344.

The Joyful

The Annunciation begins the journey in humility, "Hail, full of grace, the Lord is with you."[193]

The Visitation shows us the love of neighbor, "Most blessed are you among women, and blessed is the fruit of your womb."[194]

The Nativity of our Lord celebrates the birth of Jesus and the poverty in spirit, "She wrapped Him in swaddling clothes and laid Him in a manger."[195]

The Presentation illustrates obedience, "Every male that opens the womb shall be consecrated to the Lord."[196]

Finding of the Child Jesus in the Temple gives us the Joy of finding Jesus, "After three days they found Him in the temple, sitting in the midst of the teachers."[197]

The Luminous

The Baptism of Jesus opens the door to the Holy Spirit, "This is My beloved Son, with whom I am well pleased."[198]

The Wedding at Cana opens a path to Jesus through Mary, "His mother said to the servers, 'Do whatever He tells you.'"[199]

Proclaiming the Kingdom teaches repentance and trust in God, "As you go, make this proclamation: 'The kingdom of heaven is at hand.'"[200]

The Transfiguration gives us the desire for holiness, "Then from the cloud came a voice that said, 'This is My chosen Son; listen to Him.'"[201]

The Institution of the Eucharist is adoration of our Lord, "This is My body, which will be given for you."[202]

---

[193] Lk 1:28.
[194] Lk 1:41-42.
[195] Lk 2:7.
[196] Lk 2.22-23.
[197] Lk 2:46.

[198] Mt 3:16-17.
[199] Jn 2.5.
[200] Mt 10:7-8.
[201] Lk 9: 29,35.
[202] Lk 22:19-20.

The Sorrowful

The Agony in the Garden is aligned with our sorrow for sin, "He was in such agony and He prayed so fervently that His sweat became like drops of blood falling on the ground."[203]

The Scourging at the Pillar teaches purity and the will of God, "Then Pilate took Jesus and had Him scourged."[204]

The Crowning with Thorns shows us courage, "Weaving a crown out of thorns, they placed it on His head, and a reed in His right hand."[205]

The Carrying of the Cross teaches patience, "And carrying the cross Himself, He went out to what is called the Place of the Skull, in Hebrew, Golgotha."[206]

The Crucifixion shows perseverance, "Jesus cried out in a loud voice, 'Father, into Your hands I commend My spirit'; and when He had said this He breathed His last."[207]

The Glorious

The Resurrection is our reward for faith, "Do not be amazed! You seek Jesus of Nazareth, the crucified. He has been raised; He is not here. Behold the place where they laid Him."[208]

The Ascension is our hope, "So then the Lord Jesus, after He spoke to them, was taken up into heaven and took His seat at the right hand of God."[209]

The Decent of the Holy Spirit illustrates the love of God, "And they were all filled with the Holy Spirit and began to speak in different tongues, as the Spirit enabled them to proclaim."[210]

The Assumption is the grace of a happy death, "You are the glory of Jerusalem! You are the great boast of our nation! You have done good things for Israel, and God is pleased with them. May the

---

[203] Lk 22;44-45.
[204] Jn 19:1.
[205] Mt 27:28-29.
[206] Jn 19:17.

[207] Lk 23:46.
[208] Mk 16:6.
[209] Mk 16:19.
[210] Acts 2:4.

Almighty Lord bless you forever!"[211]

The Coronation of Mary helps our trust in Mary's intercession, "A great sign appeared in the sky, a woman clothed with the sun, with the moon under her feet, and on her head a crown of twelve stars."[212]

One of my favorite quotes heard often on the golf course is: "A bad day on the golf course, beats a good day at work – any day". A *walk in the garden of Jesus with Mary,* is there a better, more fruitful fair*way* to Heaven? A walk in the Garden, indeed.

---

[211] Jud 15:9-10.
[212] Rev 12:1.

Did You Know?

According to Fr. Calloway, there have been more than 500 Marian apparitions just in the 20th century alone. "An unprecedented number of them have been approved, some have been condemned, and the vast majority remain under investigation by the local bishop or a Vatican commission."[213] Fr. Calloway emphasizes, "When speaking of apparitions, it is always important to emphasize that no Catholic is bound to believe in private revelation. What is required for our salvation has been given to us in Public Revelation (that is, Sacred Scripture and Tradition). This does not mean, however, that the private revelations approved by the Church are unimportant."[214]

The Catechism goes even further in clarifying the proper disposition of apparitions:

"Throughout the ages, there have been so-called "private" revelations, some of which have been recognized by the authority of the Church. They do not belong, however, to the deposit of faith. It is not their role to improve or complete Christ's definitive Revelation, but to help live more fully by it in a certain period of history."[215]

Did you know that a common thread within nearly all of these Marian apparitions is the emphasis on praying the rosary? For example, "at Fatima, the Queen of Heaven sought to bring the rosary into the daily life of the Christian."[216] Our Blessed Mother's role in our salvation journey is oftentimes misunderstood, but Venerable Archbishop Fulton Sheen paints a beautiful image of her role with this quote:

"God who made the sun, also made the moon. The moon does not take away from the brilliance of the sun. All its light is reflected from the sun. The Blessed Mother reflects her Divine Son; without Him, she is nothing. With Him, she is the Mother of men."[217]

When we pair Mary's emphasis on praying the rosary with her intercessory advice at the wedding at Cana, can we assume her

---

[213] Donald H. Calloway, MIC, *Champions of the Rosary*, (Marian Press,2016), 143.

[214] Ibid., 142.

[215] CCC ¶ 67.

[216] Donald H. Calloway, MIC, *Champions of the Rosary*, (Marian Press,2016), 143.

[217] Fulton Sheen, *Reflective Light on Mary and the Moon*, bethelightofChrist.org, May 23, 2020.

proclamations reflect the will of God? Hmm, I think we can!

Final Putt

For the last several years, during my journey, I've encountered several meaningful and memorable phrases that have hit home for me.

The first phrase comes directly from our Blessed Mother in John 2:5 – "Do whatever He tells you." This verse is my all-time favorite in the Bible. Mary's last recorded words in Scripture hold profound meaning and guidance for my life. It's easy to get caught up in the stress and pressure of worldly problems, to get lost in temptation, and to lose a sense of direction and purpose. I need only to remember these words and put them into action, and my journey is back on track.

More recently, "Poco a Poco" – little by little – is part of a phrase invoked often by Fr. Mark-Mary. This phrase works on so many levels in my faith journey. It articulates how God leads us to faith – little by little. It also summarizes the end of our journey – little by little – we will arrive.

The last phrase is, *"Nunc Coepi,"* Now I begin. As mentioned before, former NFL quarterback Philip Rivers includes this phrase in many of his inspirational speeches. It comes from a larger quote attributed to Venerable Bruno Lanteri, "If I should fall even a thousand times a day, a thousand times, with peaceful repentance, I will say immediately, Nunc Coepi [Now I begin]". This is a wonderful thought to recall, each and every time we get tripped up on the journey.

So, as we continue the journey toward the target, I am mindful of Carolyn's wish, "I just want to be good at this", some of the best advice given, or received, is found when you put all three of these phrases together:

Little by little…
Do whatever He tells you.
Now I begin!

Abbreviations

Gen	Genesis
Ex	Exodus
Lev	Leviticus
Deut	Deuteronomy
Judges	Judges
1 Kgs	1 Kings
Jud	Judith
Is	Isaiah
Mt	Matthew
Mk	Mark
Lk	Luke
Jn	John
Acts	Acts of the Apostles
Rom	Romans
2 Cor	2 Corinthians
Gal	Galatians
1 Th	1 Thessalonians
Heb	Hebrews
Rev	Revelation
CCC	Catechism of the Catholic Church
GS	Gaudium et Spes

About the Author

R.J. Gilson is a lifelong Catholic, a frequent golfer, and passionate writer who enjoys blending faith with the game he loves.

Inspired by a Bible study on the Sacraments, he set out to create a book that would serve as a lasting spiritual legacy for his children and others seeking a deeper understanding of their Catholic faith. Drawing from personal experiences, humor, and years of reflection, Gilson weaves a narrative that is both educational and entertaining. Through Fairway to Heaven, he hopes to inspire readers to appreciate the beauty of Catholicism—both on and off the golf course.

Made in the USA
Middletown, DE
14 September 2025